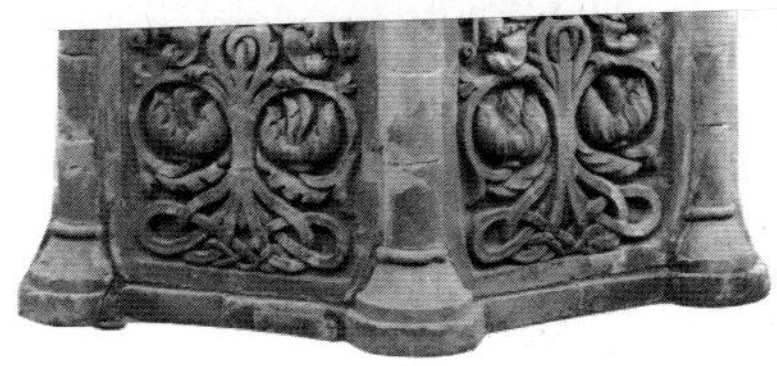

*'A piece of terracotta
wrought by human hand
is worth all the stone in Carrara
cut by machinery'*

JOHN RUSKIN
Seven Lamps of Architecture,
1849

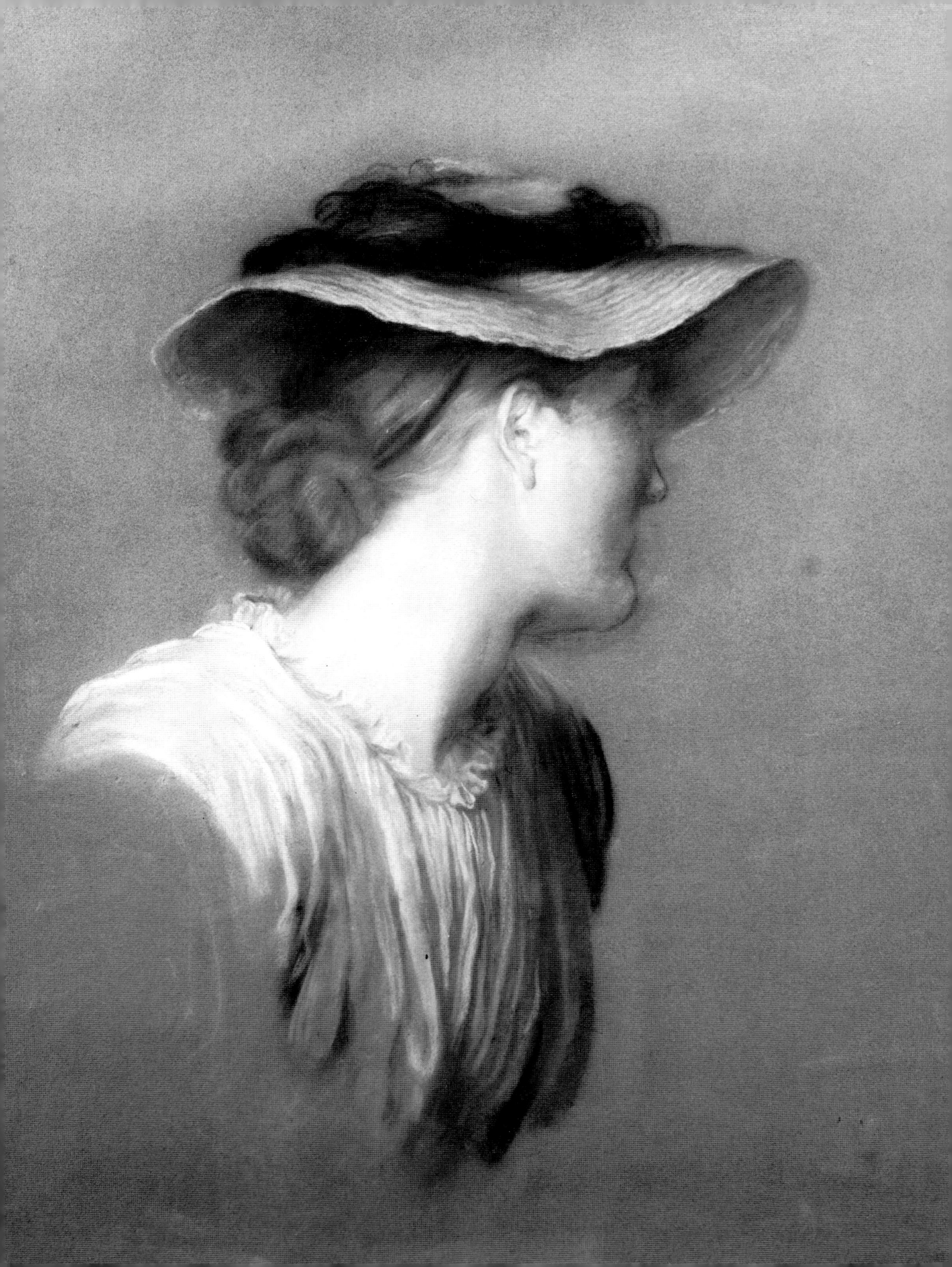

Veronica Franklin Gould

MARY SETON WATTS (1849-1938)

Unsung Heroine of the Art Nouveau

With contributions by

Richard Ormond, Richard Jefferies,

Lucinda Lambton and Barbara Morris

THE WATTS GALLERY

Published by Veronica Franklin Gould
For the Trustees of the Watts Gallery for the
Mary Watts Centenary Exhibition
5 June – 6 September 1998

Typeset in Bembo and printed by
BAS Printers, Over Wallop
Distributed by Lund Humphries Publishers Ltd

ISBN 0 9515811 2 0

Illustrated on cover
Our Lady of the Snows (detail), 1906

Illustrated on half-title page
Wellhead, 1906

Illustrated opposite title page
GEORGE FREDERIC WATTS:
Mary Seton Watts, oil on canvas, 1886

Illustrated on contents page
Celtic Pot, terracotta, 1899

Illustrated on back cover
Altarpiece from Cambridge Military Chapel, Aldershot (detail), 1915–21

Contents

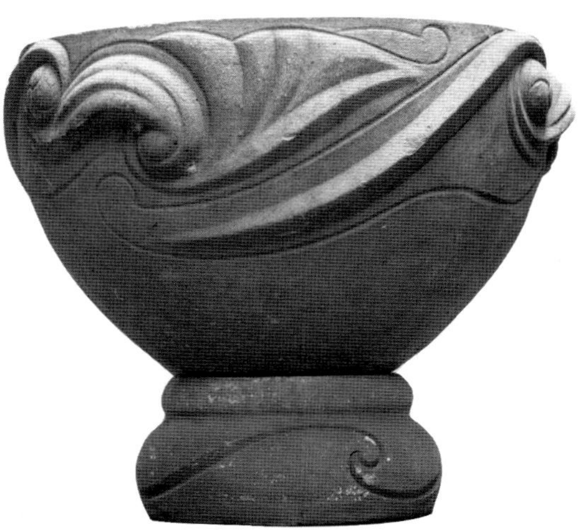

Trustees of the Watts Gallery

Exhibition Patrons

Colonel Angus Cameron
Mrs Ronald Chapman
John Christian
Richard Dorment
David Dunhill
Lady Anne Erskine
Professor Sir Andrew Huxley
Lucinda Lambton
Michael More Molyneux
Barbara Morris
Richard Ormond
Peter Rose
Tim Seago
Peyton Skipwith
Baron Sweerts de Landas Wyborgh
Viscount de Vesci

Donors

Martin Beisly
John and Margie Christian
Christie's
Richard Dennis
Lady Anne Erskine
Esmée Fairburn Charitable Trust
Farnham Art Society
The Marc Fitch Fund
Colin and Charlotte Franklin Charitable Trust
Jill Franklin Trust
The David and Myrtle FranklinTrust
J Paul Getty Jnr Charitable Trust
Guildford Borough Council
Messrs Hoare & Co
Jane Hollond
The Interbuild Fund
Loseley
Peter Nahum at the Leicester Galleries
Richard Ormond
Bernard Sunley Charitable Foundation
Surrey County Council
Surrey Historic Buildings Trust
Doreen Trudel

Sponsors

AIR CANADA

Transport of *Our Lady of the Snows*, *The Queen's Banner*

PEW CORNER

Exhibition Display

Foreword

The Watts Chapel is recognised as one of the masterpieces of Art Nouveau architecture. Mary Seton Watts, long overshadowed by her celebrated husband George Frederic Watts, was herself an influential artist. Her Arts and Crafts designs in terracotta, textiles, bookbindings and architecture represented England, Scotland and Ireland in International exhibitions at the turn of the century and her Potters' Arts Guild continued decades after her death. The Trustees of the Watts Gallery are delighted that Veronica Franklin Gould, who has been researching the life and work of Mary Watts, has prepared the exhibition and catalogue for reassessment of a remarkable creative figure.

We are indebted to patrons, donors and lenders – institutions and generous private individuals – for making the exhibition possible. Our thanks go to Colonel Angus Cameron, Theresa Chapman, John de Trafford, Audrey Draper, Colin Franklin, Nigel Franklin, Peter Hannen, Lionel Jebb, Sir John Leslie, Liberty plc., Christina May, Rosalind Melville, Charles Sebag-Montefiore, Belinda Norman Butler, Tony Peart, Tim and Lindy Seago, Dolf Sweerts de Landas and Chris Tuckwell. We are grateful to Lucinda Lambton and Barbara Morris, to Keith Baker, Michael Barker, Dr Elizabeth Cumming, John Christian, Hamish Dewar, Richard Dorment, Dr Nicola Gordon Bowe, Cindy Gould, Chris Lovell, Katherine Morton, Peter Nahum, Peter Rose, Peyton Skipwith, Charles Marsden Smedley, Sotheby's Garden Statuary Department, Tadema Gallery, Kate Knowles, Dr Eric Turner, the Tate Gallery Press Office, and a special acknowledgement to Meg Botting. Finally, we thank Richard Jefferies, Curator of the Watts Gallery, Janet Maclean and Juliette Gawade, and our generous sponsors Air Canada and Pew Corner.

RICHARD ORMOND

Chairman of the Trustees of the Watts Gallery

Emerging from the Shadows

Mary Fraser Tytler's marriage to George Frederic Watts in 1886 coincided with his rising reputation as one of the most influential and revered painters. A gifted and original artist herself, the Scotswoman 33 years his junior, directed the new dimension in her life for the benefit of others.

As the handicraft revival took hold all over the land, astounded peasantry began to pot and weave in classes run by the Home Arts and Industries Association. Mary, a Home Arts activist, believed passionately that anyone given the opportunity could produce things of beauty, and thus it was that a village ploughboy received as much encouragement and guidance as a lady of leisure.

When the exotic vegetation of Art Nouveau first took tentative root in Britain, Mary pruned the abandoned writhings of the Continental parent and grafted on to it the more constrained and disciplined decoration of her Celtic heritage. Her belief in universality required that the new hybrid should also be budded with snippets of Egyptian, Indian and Assyrian decoration. Her unique style gained wide recognition, and award-winning terracotta garden ornaments produced by her Potters' Arts Guild and favoured by Gertrude Jekyll were in demand everywhere.

To celebrate the centenary of the dedication of the remarkable Watts Chapel, other facets of Mary's oeuvre, hitherto overlooked, have been gathered together for the first time to show the broad range of her achievements and what she enabled others to achieve. At last Mary Watts emerges from the shadows of her own reticence and her husband's fame into her rightful place as a wielding force in the Arts and Crafts Movement.

RICHARD JEFFERIES
Curator of the Watts Gallery

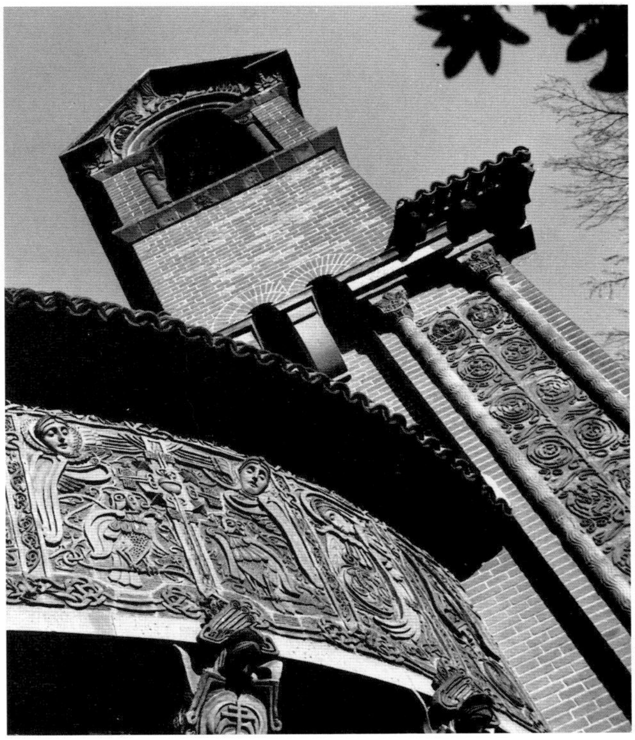

An Architectural Jewel

LUCINDA LAMBTON

Driving on the A3 south of Guildford, on no account look East. The mere sight of the Watts Chapel will send you spinning off the road with delight. A brilliant beacon of a building – seemingly aflame with the redness of its brick – that has been most surprisingly wrought into the ancient forms of a Greek cross with Romanesque motifs and a cacophony of Celtic decoration.

It was designed and decorated by Mary Watts – wife of the great Victorian painter G F Watts – who had never built anything before in her life. She had in fact hoped that it would eventually blend into the countryside but it most certainly does not, never will and is all the more glorious because of that.

In 1895 Mrs Watts designed a chapel for the new burial ground in Compton, Surrey, and started pottery classes at her home near by, teaching the villagers to model its clay tiles, while Watts painted pictures to pay for it. All hands were plunged forthwith into producing the intricate work, and within three years the exterior of the chapel was finished for its dedication.

Everyone an amateur, with the exception of the blacksmith, the local builder, a carpenter and an architect called Redmayne – who supervised Mary Watts supervising the workforce – the whole village was said to be involved in the chapel's creation. What richly satisfying rewards they reaped for their

The Watts Chapel
Compton

efforts! Still as blindingly brilliant as the day it was built, it is scarcely possible to believe that such a sight is set before your eyes on a green hill in Surrey.

Four great terracotta friezes of Celtic encrustations – convoluted carvings symbolizing Hope, Love, Truth and Light – sweep round on curved walls between the arms of the cross – 'The Circle of Eternity with the Cross of Faith running through it'. Crossed-winged angels support the friezes: symbols of Life, Truth and the Way, while over the arched doorway there is a choir of angels, their wings pierced with the eye of the peacock – symbol of watchfulness. The building is indeed saturated with symbolism – every inch a message from Mrs Watts – all of it sensational beauty.

Inside you are straightway enfolded by the glow of dark and richly subtle tones, with the endlessly interweaving lines of Celtic knots untangling and retangling themselves in and out of swirling Art Nouveau forms – 'woven' according to Mary Watts 'as it were into a mystical garment'. Worked in gesso – fibre soaked in plaster of Paris – every line is in either exquisitely sharp or softly bulging relief. With such a wealth of writing, the walls seem alive with vigour. The Tree of Life grows forth, its branches flowering into symbolic cameos, whilst the roots flow beneath the 'Winged Messengers' – great feathered giantesses of mesmerising beauty who stand two by two around the chapel walls 'presenting the light and the dark side of all things': Those of the light have haunting faces gazing out at you, those of the dark, their backs turned. Gilded capitals support thickly vaulted ribs, emblazoned with life-sized cherub's faces that soar heavenward, past crimson clad seraphs blessing the winged giantesses below.

The effect of the chapel on your senses is startling. I have yet to see one who is not left breathless with wonder when standing within its walls.

If a jewel were to be set into Britain's architectural crown, none would be more splendidly suitable than the Chapel created by Mary Watts.

Liberty's Pioneer Designer

BARBARA MORRIS

Arthur Lasenby Liberty (1843-1917) told his artist friends that if he had a shop of his own he would change the whole look of fashion in dress and decoration. When his Regent Street store opened in 1875, initially selling imported Eastern goods, it was patronized by artists and devotees of 'art for art's sake' and became a focus for the Aesthetic Movement. From the 1880s, he began to commission textiles and other objects from the leading architects and designers of the day.

Although Liberty, who moved in both artistic and establishment circles, would almost certainly have known G F Watts, it was through Mary's friendship with James Morton (1867-1923), son of Liberty's main producer of the woven furnishing fabrics – Alexander Morton and Company of Darvel – that she become involved with Liberty's. She designed his first Celtic-style carpet and encouraged him to 'carry forward the Celtic art'. To Mary, Morton was her 'knight of commerce', who sympathized with her Home Arts and Industries Association interests, found her first professional Compton pottery manager and helped negotiate sales. In gratitude, Watts painted a portrait of James as a wedding gift on his marriage in 1900 to Beatrice Fagan.

Celtic motifs were to feature prominently in Liberty's products around the turn of the century, introduced mainly through the influence of John Llewellyn, who joined Liberty's in 1889 becoming a director in 1898. Responsible for the textiles department, he also introduced the 'Cymric' and 'Tudric' ranges of silver and pewter with their entrelac and other Celtic-inspired motifs designed by Archibald Knox, who like Mary designed Donegal carpets and garden furniture for Liberty's. A passion for

Celtic art was evidently a bond between the two Scots, James Morton and Mary Watts, the Welshman John Llewellyn and the Manxman Archibald Knox.

In 1898 Alexander Morton & Company, in co-operation with the Congested Districts Board, set up a workshop at Killybegs in County Donegal to produce hand-knotted rugs and carpets employing local female labour, later further factories were established at Kilcar, Crololy and Anagry employing altogether some 500 girls. The rugs and carpets were known as 'Donegal' and James Morton invited Mary to make designs for them, developing her new living version of ancient Celtic forms. These Donegal carpets were taken up by Liberty's and shown in March 1903 in their exhibition entitled *Founding a National Industry – Irish Carpets* at the Grafton Gallery. Mary's *Pelican* rug (1899, see pages 52-53) and her garden pottery were among the exhibits. Although it was not Liberty's practice to acknowledge the source of their designs – not even such internationally famed names as C F A Voysey and Christopher Dresser – uniquely Mary's name appeared in the

Cobra and Hanging Pots at Liberty's Irish carpet exhibition, 1903

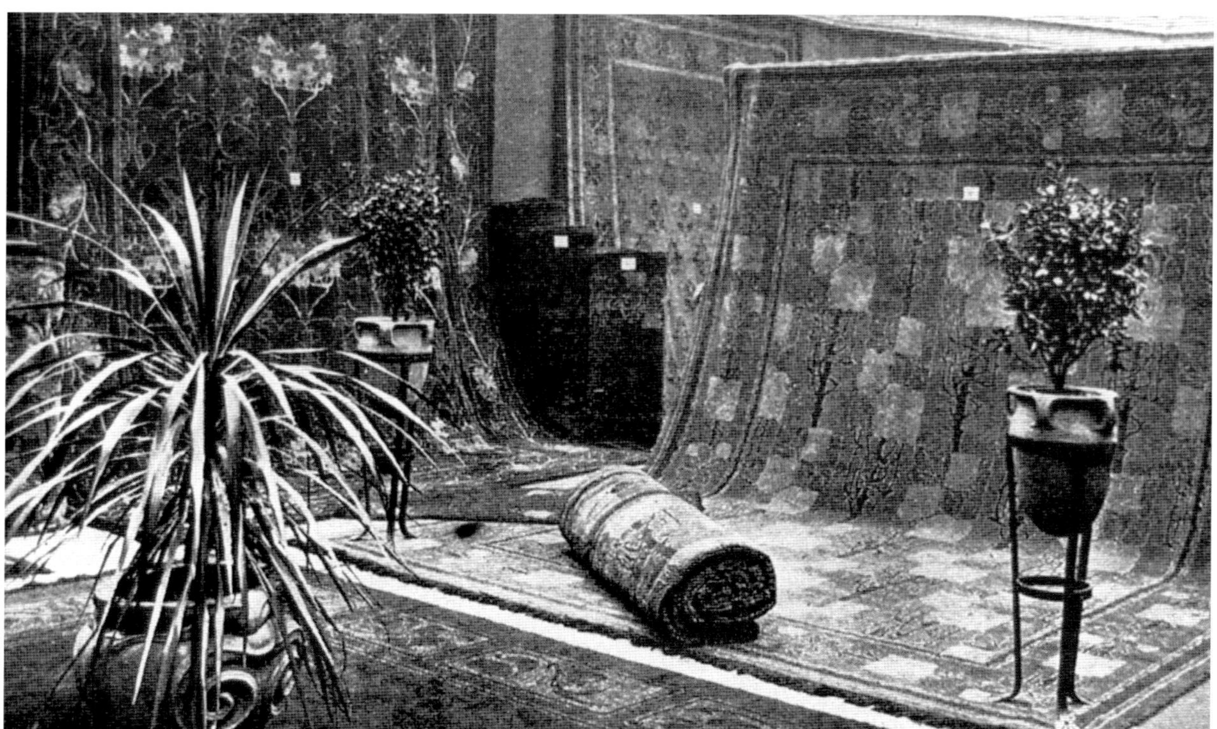

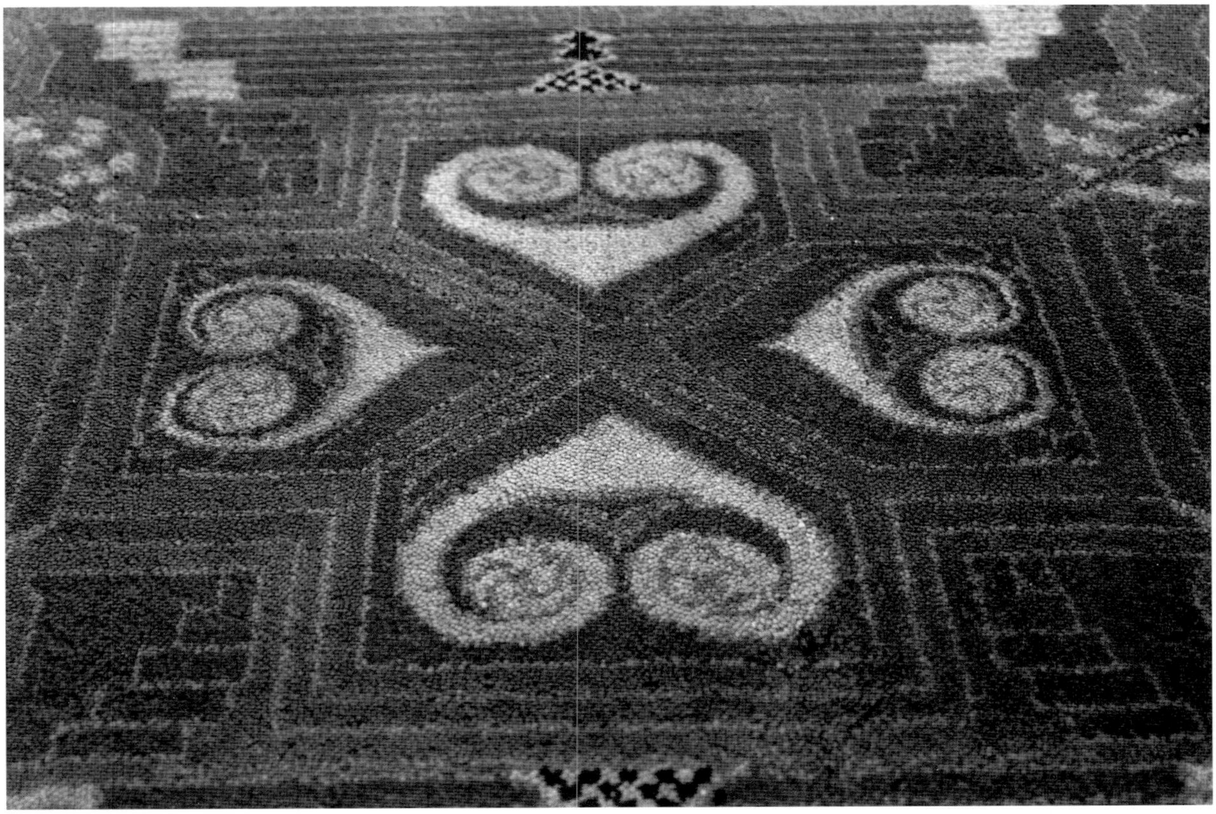

Cat 43. The Pelican carpet, hand-tufted for Alexander Morton & Co, at Killibegs, 1899-1901. Detail

catalogue – a distinction rare. The carpets were highly praised in *The Studio* (Vol 28, 286) and *The Furniture Record* (Vol VIII, 1903, 251) declared that the carpets 'have marked and distinctive characteristics in design and colouring which will probably lead to making the carpet the starting point of the decoration of a room.'

The following March Liberty's held an exhibition of *Modern Celtic Art* including gold and silver plate, jewellery, carpets and garden pottery, the latter mostly designed by Mary. Her work featured prominently in Liberty's *Book of Garden Ornaments* (1904) whose introduction stated that 'as in other branches of the applied arts, the present exhibitors have struck out into untrodden paths and in this instance largely aided and advised by Mrs G F Watts, the talented wife of our greatest living artist, have shown us what notable results can be achieved by simple forms treated with bold designs.' The Liberty garden pottery received Gold and Silver medals from both the Royal Botanic Society and the Royal Horticultural Society. Although not acknowledged, Archibald Knox was responsible for some of the garden pottery and others were produced by Carter & Company at Poole. The 1906 *Studio Year Book of Decorative Art* included a section on 'Garden Furniture' (247-276), illustrating seven items designed by Mary and executed by her Potters' Arts Guild and four 'designed and executed by Liberty & Company'. Not credited to any designer, less curvaceous and with more pointed interlaced forms than Mary's, the latter – like a number of Liberty terracotta garden ornaments continuing into the 1920s – may well have been made at the Compton pottery founded by this pioneering craftswoman.

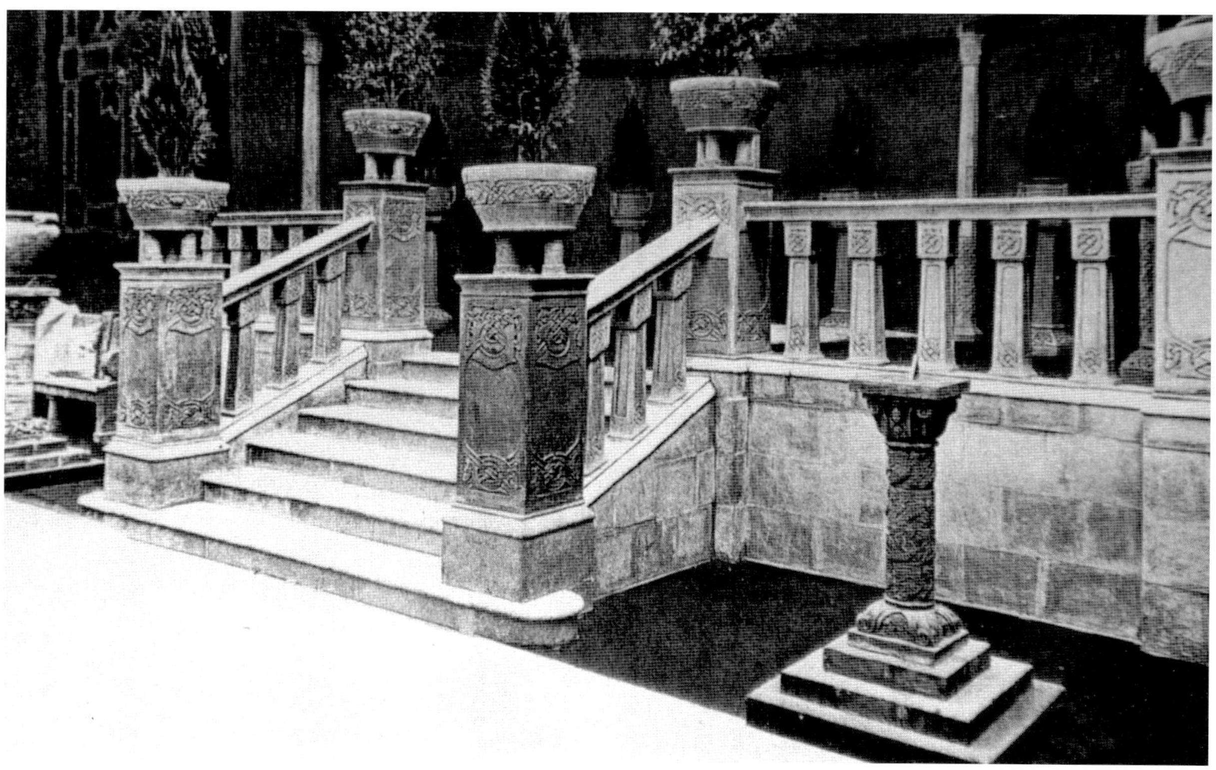

The Winged Hours sundial on the right and Scroll Pot on the left, in the Gold Medal display, illustrated in Liberty's Garden Pottery catalogue, 1905

Chronology

1849
Mary Seton Fraser Tytler, third daughter of Charles Edward Fraser Tytler and Etheldred (née St Barbe), born at Ahmednaggar, India, 25 November

1851
Brought up at Aldourie, grandparents' Highland estate in Inverness-shire

1861
Moves to Sanquhar, Forres when father retires from Indian Civil service

1868-70
Freshwater, Isle of Wight, makes props and sits for photographer Julia Margaret Cameron. Studies art in Dresden and Rome

1870
Kensington. First visit to studio of George Frederic Watts, Little Holland House, enrols at South Kensington Art Training School. Paints Christina Fraser Tytler

1872-73
Studies at The Slade

c 1874
Studies with Aimée-Jules Dalou

1875
Freshwater, paints Ethel Fraser Tytler. Growing friendship with Watts

1876
Edinburgh, portrait painted by George Paul Chalmers, SRA. Becomes Watts's student

1877
Portraits of Christina and Eleanor

1881-82
Father dies. Self-Portraits, portrait of Mary Eden

1884
Starts clay-modelling class for Whitechapel shoeblacks

1885
First annual exhibition of the Home Arts and Industries Association.

1886
Marries Watts Saturday 20 November

1887
Plans to design bas-reliefs decorations to symbolize Wattsian thought. Studies anatomy with Henry Moore, photography with W J Stillman and Frederic Hollyer. Burne-Jones arranges instruction in *gesso duro* from Osmund Weeks. First gesso decoration, Watts's reading alcove at LHH. He paints three portraits of his wife. Council members of the South London Fine Art Gallery and Home Arts and Industries Association

1888
'The Utmost for the Highest' motif

1889
Refuses Sir Frederic Leighton's invitation to sign anti-female suffrage letter. Cast of the Watts' hands

1890-91
Limnerslease, built by Ernest George at Compton, Surrey. Mary designs symbolic gesso ceiling as memorial to Watts, consults Walter Crane. Studies ancient civilizations. Marchioness of Waterford's memorial cross, clay relief of *Death Crowning Innocence*

1893
Reading alcove and fire surround at Limnerslease, reredos for St Albans workhouse chapel. Visits Conrad Dressler's studio, encourages his Della Robbia ceramic workshop scheme, notes 'Germ of my Potters Work'

1894-95
Watts' unofficially adopt 13-year-old Lilian Mackintosh. Plans to teach Compton villagers to make terracotta gravestones. Spearheads Home Arts fund-raising campaign, *The Epsom Beggar.* Offer to design mortuary chapel accepted by Compton Parish Council. Model of chapel completed August 1895. Brick model built by George Barrow and Albert Boxall. First clay-modelling classes for chapel decoration at Limnerslease

1896
Compton Terra Cotta Home Arts exhibits chapel capitals at Royal Albert Hall. Path of the Just friezes and doorway. *Hand and Soul*

1897
Louis Deuchars assists pottery class

1898
Architect George Redmayne refines chapel hinges. Plans to establish professional pottery business. Sundials, Art Nouveau seats, Scroll Pot. Chapel dedicated by Bishop of Winchester on 1 July. Inverness-shire. Consults Phoebe Traquair. *Cuir bouilli* bookbinding for Guild of Women-Binders. *The Word in the Pattern*

1899
Chapel altar in Home Arts exhibition at Royal Albert Hall. Inverness-shire. *Pelican* Donegal carpet for Alexander Morton & Co

1900–01
Watts' sundial at Home Arts exhibition, cottage plaque. Starts pottery at Aldourie. Compton's first pottery manager James Nicol. Carpets and terracotta in Irish Pavilion at Glasgow International Exhibition. Queen Victoria memorial Sundial. Watts's studio fireplace. Exhibits bedhead at Home Arts

1902
Commissioned by Irish Department of Agriculture and Technical Instruction to make architectural and garden ornaments. Tom Wren head modeller at Compton. *Lovat Scouts Casket* carried out by Louis Deuchars. Bookbinding *Thomas à Kempus* made by F Gertrude Farran in Arts and Crafts Exhibition Society exhibition

1903
Pelican Donegal carpet and terracotta exhibited in Liberty's *Founding a National Industry*, Grafton Gallery Christopher Turnor builds combined Watts Gallery and hostel for apprentice potters

1904
Exhibits for Ireland at St Louis World's Fair and in Liberty's *Modern Celtic Art*, Grafton Gallery. Liberty's *Book of Garden Ornaments.* Chapel interior completed. Death of Watts 1 July. Models flower for his statue of *Tennyson*. Celtic birdbath, *His Pilgrims Way*. Potteries named 'The Potters' Arts Guild'. Large wheelmark for terracotta and small 'PAG' wheelmark for decorative coloured ware

1905
Brass altar set for All Saints, Ennismore Gardens

1906–7
Wellheads, drinking fountain, *Our Lady of the Snows* banner presented by Queen Alexandra to McGill University and *The Spirit of the Flowers of the Nations* banner for Government House, Ottawa. *The Word in the Pattern* bookbinding by F Gertrude Farran in A&C Ex Soc exhibition. *Gospel at Work* bookbinding. President of Women's Guild of Arts. RHS silver medals for terracotta

1909
Princess of Wales visits. Memorials to Eleanor Kellie Maccallum Dalgleish and Patrick Fraser Tytler.

1910
Terracotta commission from architect Herbert Baker. Potters' Arts Guild wins Home Arts' gold cross

1912–13
Royal International Horticultural Society silver medal

1916–21
Aldershot military chapel. Compton War Memorial. Miniature pots for Queen Mary's Dolls House

1923
Fire destroys thatched pottery building. Rebuilt

1936
Compton Potters' Arts Guild becomes limited company, George Aubertin as manager

1938
Dies 6 September 1938

1950–55
Pottery bought by David Dunhill, features Aubertin on BBC *Interlude*. Pottery closes 1955

Unsung Heroine of the Art Nouveau

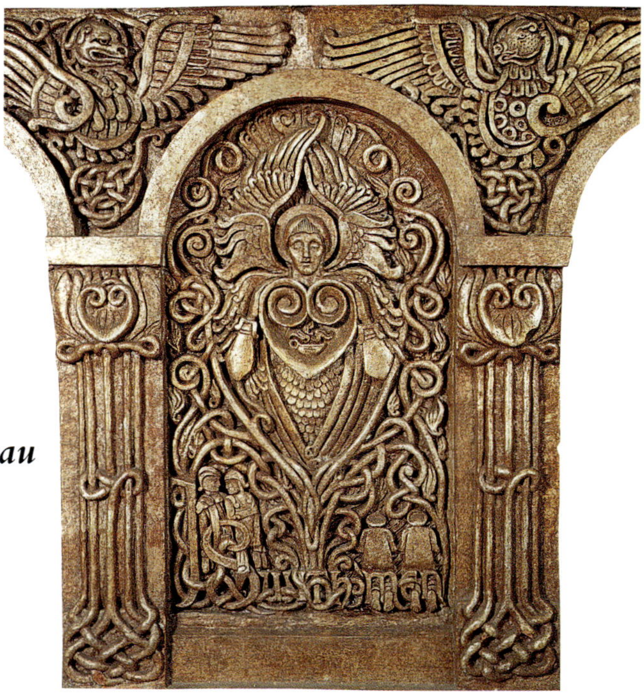

VERONICA FRANKLIN GOULD

'How glad I am that you are going to *carry forward* the Celtic art,' 'It is our own, & was left incomplete – I love it with all my heart,' Mary Watts wrote to the textile manufacturer James Morton. 'We in the present day should not be mere *copyists* of their elaborate knottings or half thought out, though beautiful & original designs, but breathe its spirit and work upon the same lines ... use it as a language in which our modern thoughts can be conveyed, *invent* upon it ... There is no decorative art so suited for *telling* its story.'[1]

Celtic passion was the key to Mary's creativity, released like an uncoiled spring or La Tène spiral[2] when, at nearly 37, after a love-lorn spinsterhood she married George Frederic Watts, the British Symbolist and premier portrait-painter. She abandoned easel painting and began to design symbolic bas-reliefs; and while he painted poetic ideas on canvas, she became an extraordinary modeller of ideas. In his lack of decoration and her contrasting

Above: The Watts Chapel, 1901-4
Detail of interior

extensive use of pantheistic symbolism, both sought to uplift and relate to people of all nations through their art.

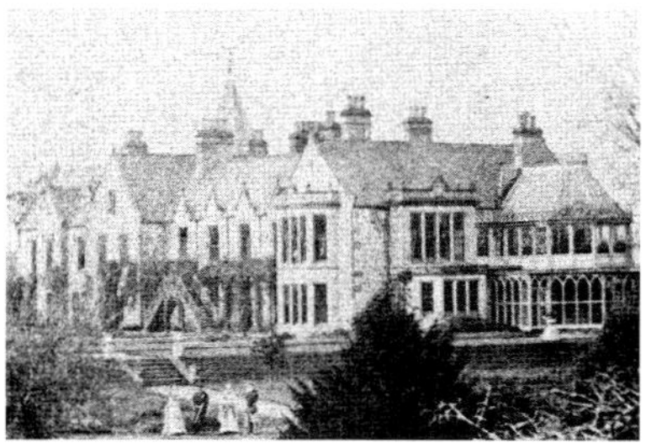

Sanquhar

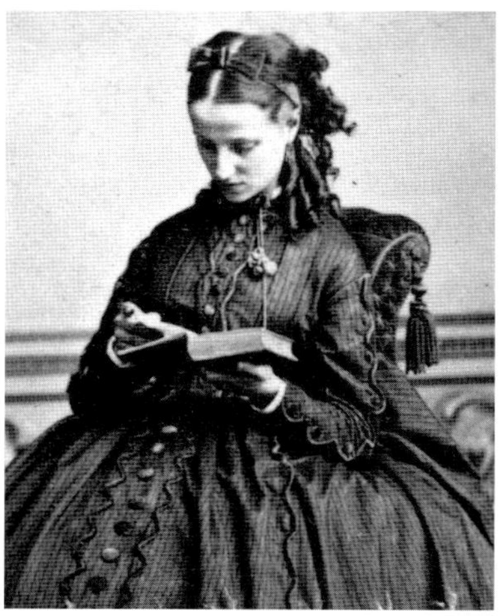

Mary Fraser Tytler

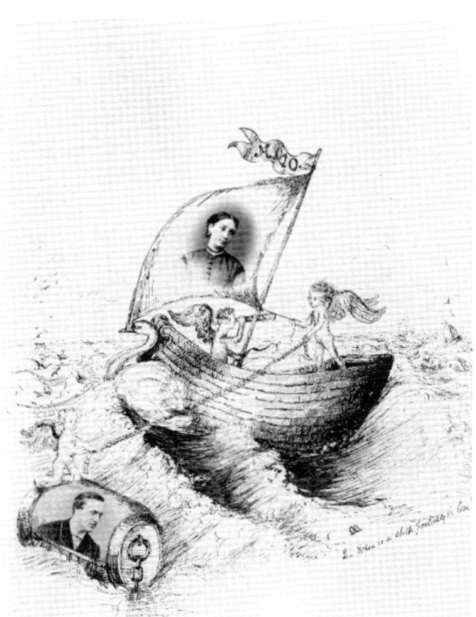

'When is a ship foolishly in love?'

Mary Seton Fraser Tytler was born on 25 November 1849 at Ahmednaggar in India, where her father Charles worked for the Honourable East India Company's Civil Service. Her mother Etheldred (née St Barbe) died when Mary, her third daughter, was eighteen months old and the girls were brought up by their grandparents at Aldourie Castle, near Dores, Inverness-shire where William Fraser Tytler served as Sheriff-Depute for 42 years. Sir Walter Scott had been a friend of his father Lord Woodhouselee, who had edited Burns' poems, and of his brother Patrick Fraser Tytler, author of the classic *History of Scotland* (1826-43).

Conscious of her links with the literary soul of Scotland, Mary was educated at home by governesses. Her family moved to Sanquhar, near Forres when Charles returned from India with his second wife in 1861. While her father amused himself writing esoteric dissertations on *The Structure of Prophecy* and *New View of the Apocalypse*, he encouraged his daughters to pursue their poetic and artistic interests. Mary embraced the Victorian vogue for decorating photograph albums with imaginative watercolour settings for *cartes-de visite*. Her delight in nature and ornament stands out from the pages. Glimpses of family and friends in 1867-68 show a baronet transformed into the petal of a pansy, croquet balls aimed at the formal images of the contestants, highland chiefs at jaunty angles in a stem of heather, and the face of a friend emerging from a boat while her suitor's head bobs on a barrel in the ocean. Enterprising use of symbolism suggests that at seventeen Mary attended the new Inverness Art Training School, when her elder sisters first sat for Julia Margaret Cameron at Dimbola, the photographer's studio at Freshwater, Isle of Wight. Mrs Cameron had insisted that they meet her 'divine artist' George Frederic Watts,[3] who lived with her sister and brother-in-law, Sara Prinsep at Little Holland House in Kensington. He had been ostracised by society after his scandalous separation from his teenage

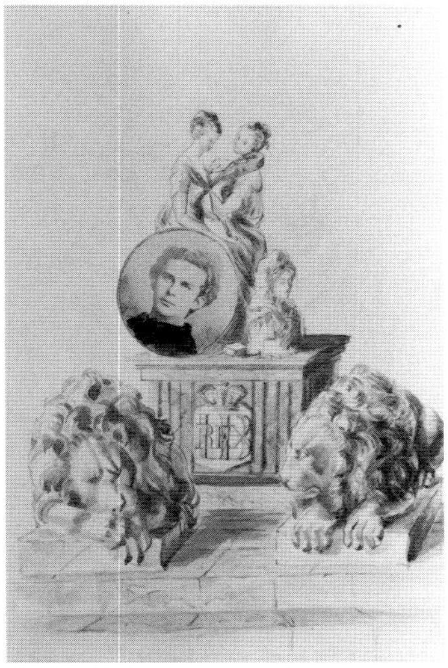

Ludwig of Bavaria

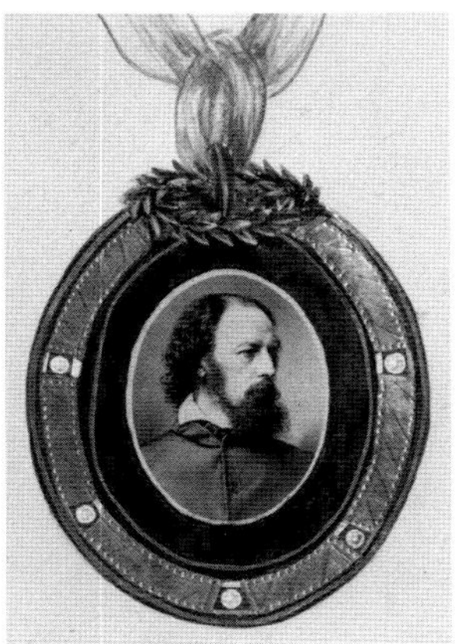

Alfred Tennyson, 1868

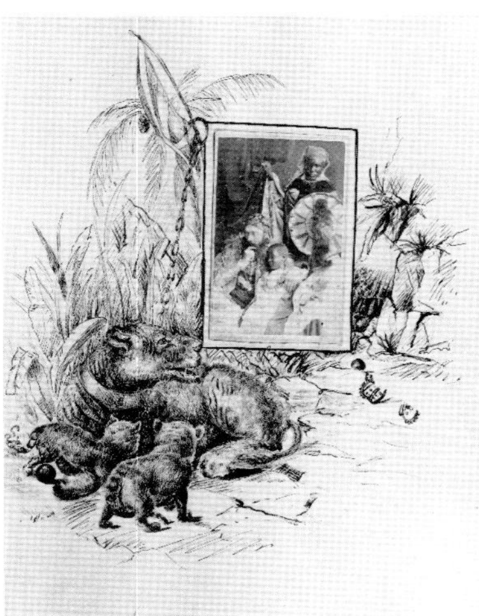

Cat 2. Prince Alamayu
Casa holds Mary's shield, 1868

bride, the actress Ellen Terry, but continued to be the centre of attraction at Mrs Prinsep's legendary salons.

Anglo-Indian links were presumably responsible for the friendship between Julia Margaret Cameron and the Fraser Tytlers. Married to the Anglo-Indian jurist Charles Hay Cameron, she was the most eccentric of the seven Indian-born Pattle sisters, who Mary reported, were 'Artistic to their finger-tips, with an appreciation – almost to be called a *culte* – for beauty'.[4] In 1863, three years after moving to Dimbola, next door to Farringford, home of the Poet Laureate, Mrs Cameron had taken up photography. As Alfred Tennyson achieved through poetry, Watts painted on to canvas the mind of the Victorian era. Julia Margaret Cameron, seeking to secure for photography the status of High Art, looked to Watts for advice. She aimed to convey qualities of his paintings, as well as those of the Raphaelites in portraits of 'famous men and fair women' taken between 1864 and 1870.

In Freshwater at that time Tennyson was composing his seminal *Idylls of the King*. It seemed to Anny Thackeray, daughter of the novelist, that 'Everybody is either a genius, or a poet, or a painter or peculiar in some way'[5] as eighteen-year-old Mary found when she spent four months there in the spring of 1898. The poet invited her to Farringford. He held her hand while he read *Maud* and walked along the shore with her in the moonlight; and she devoted the frontispiece of her new album to him, quoting from his feminist epic *The Princess* (1847), 'Our echoes roll from soul to soul / And grow for ever and for ever.'[6]

Mrs Cameron visited the Fraser Tytlers at Westover House, and the next day Mary began to make her a shield as a prop. The phographer 'commanded, and it was done', Mary recalled.[7] Her shield appears in photographs of nine-year-old Abyssinian Prince Alamayu, whose father Emperor Theodore had recently shot himself rather than surrender to the British at the Siege of Magdale. She met the boy and his guardian Captain Speedy at Dimbola, and their photograph appears in her album watched by a lioness chained to a palm-tree, and two lion cubs. Sadly three upturned horseshoes failed to bring him luck, for the prince was to die at nineteen.

Cat 1. JULIA MARGARET CAMERON, Rosebud Garden of Girls, 1868

'Queen rose of the rosebud garden of girls,
Come hither, the dances are done,
In gloss of satin and glimmer of pearls,
Queen lily and rose in one;
Shine out, little head, sunning over with curls,
To the flowers, and be their sun.

There has fallen a splendid tear
From the passion-flower at the gate,
She is coming, my dove, my dear;
She is coming, my life, my fate;
The red rose cries, 'She is near, she is near;'
And the white rose weeps, 'She is late;'
The larkspur listens, 'I hear, I hear;'
And the lily whispers, 'I wait.'

Whether friend or stranger, sitters usually had to be cajoled into enduring Julia Margaret Cameron's lens, but the Fraser Tytler girls were eager participants. On Saturday 20 June 1868, Mary and her sisters arrived at Dimbola for a group photograph inspired by Tennyson's *Maud*. Changing out of their stays into loose flowing robes, they removed pins and ribbons from their hair, and posed against a virginal backdrop of climbing roses. Each held symbolic flowers. Cameron believed no woman should be photographed between eighteen and 80, but only Eleanor was younger than eighteen. She stands on the left, looking dreamily upwards, clutching to her breast a spray of passion-flowers; next to her, seated sideways across the foreground, the poet Christina gazes to the right beyond the picture plane, a red rose, symbol of martyrdom, in her hand; Mary, her firm jawline evident despite the Cameron soft focus, sits beside Christina, a larkspur rising from the cluster of foliage and heart's tongue fern leaf in her lap; and on the far right, Ethel stands with her lilies, apprehensive, 'I wait'. In the Pre-Raphaelite *Rosebud Garden of Girls*, each girl seems to have entered into the spirit of her role in the scene they were recreating together to illustrate the combined genius of Cameron and Tennyson.

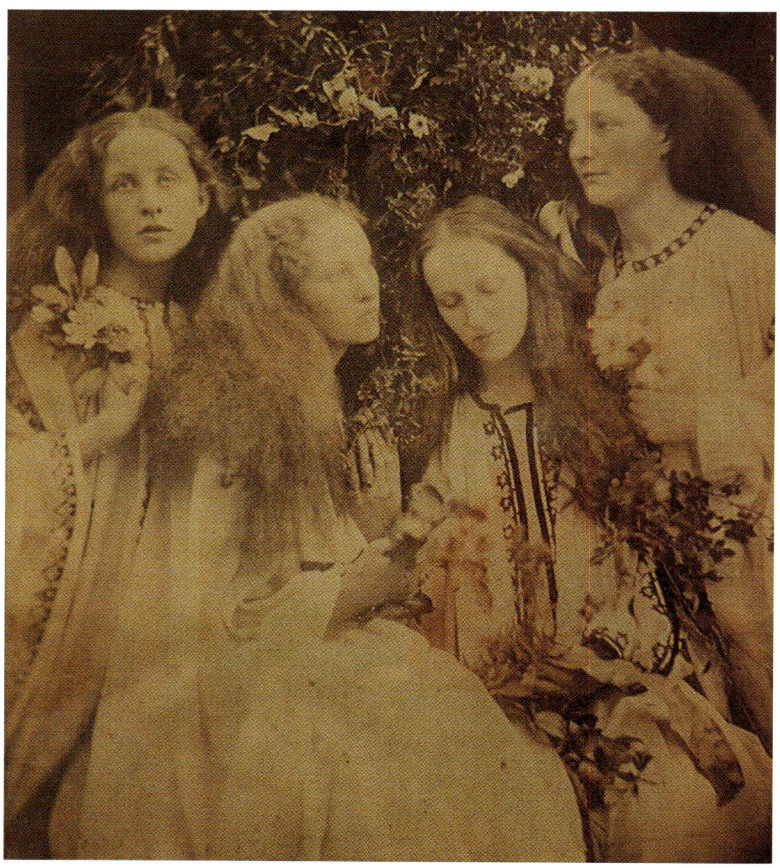

The girls' exuberant spirits returned the moment the sitting was over. Robes and hair flying, they bounded up the stairs past the poet William Allingham who was confronted by the triumphant photographer brandishing a dripping glass negative. 'Magnificent!' exclaimed Cameron. 'To focus them all in one picture, such an effort!'[8]

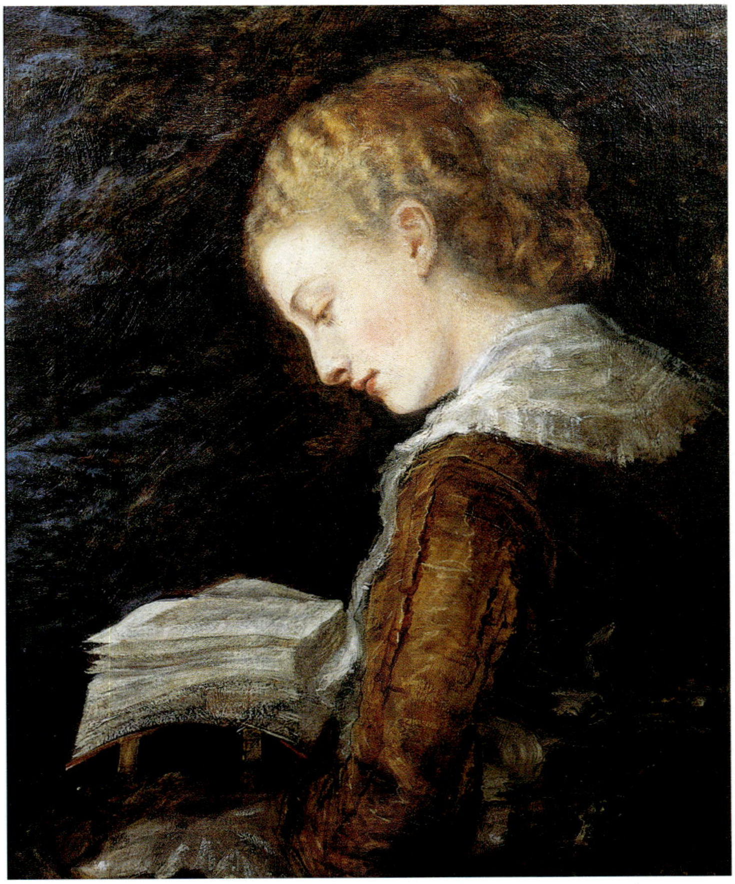

Cat 5. Christina Liddell, 1870

At the end of July the Fraser Tytlers set sail for Europe. Mary spent the winter studying art in Dresden, met the Empress of Austria and fell for her cousin, Ludwig of Bavaria. Both appear in Mary's album. A monument to the handsome young king and his muses is shown guarded by lions – one ferocious, the other dozing, bored by Ludwig's artistic and architectural enterprise. More seriously, a broken love affair in Rome caused Mary anguish for decades. She would counteract her private torment – on occasion almost suicidal – by throwing herself into painting. In a remarkable portrait in oil of Christina, she unleashed her misery into passionate paint handling of the background while her joy at her sister's engagement to Edward Liddell can be seen in the delicate treatment of Christina's face. The influence is unmistakably Wattsian, for as she later wrote in *George Frederic Watts: The Annals of an Artists' Life*, 'Now at all modern exhibitions I acknowledged to myself that George Frederic Watts was the painter of painters for me.'[9]

Mary continued her studies at the National Art Training School in South Kensington. Her father took a house near by at 9 Queensgate Place, and in the spring of 1870 she secured an invitation to meet Watts at Little Holland House. The 20-year-old embraced this opportunity to further her career – arguably the most significant step of her life – with trepidation. Chaperoned by Christina, she waited outside the Academician's studio. A notice emblazoned on the red baize door filled her with awe: 'I must beg not to be disturbed till after two o'clock.' As the door swung back,

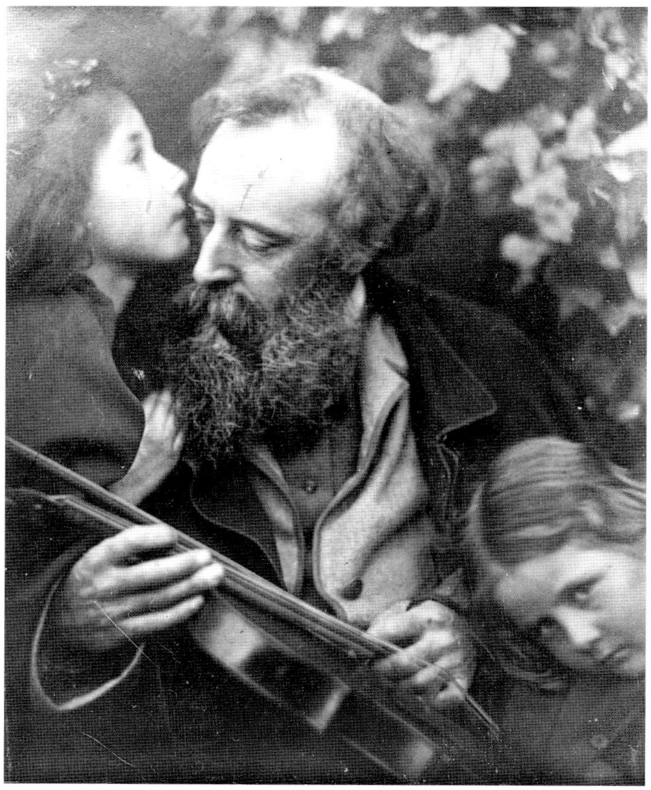

Cat 3. JULIA MARGARET CAMERON, Whisper of the Muse, 1865

'Signor [as Watts was known to friends] came forward to meet us … the beard was only slightly touched with grey, his hair quite brown, very fine in quality, and brushed back from the forehead … I remember the painter much more distinctly than his work; but he nevertheless so distinctly suggested to me the days of chivalry that I believe I should not have been surprised if, on another visit, I had found him all clad in shining armour.'[10]

In retrospect she recalled the man more than his paintings, but over the next sixteen years, their friendship in art matured as master and student, although Mary – still very much in awe of him – was one of many amateur artists to whom Watts gave guidance.[11] She thought of herself as an amateur because, although well-bred women could study art, dabble in watercolours, and even exhibit, it was socially unacceptable to turn professional or to dirty their hands with clay modelling. Yet her contemporary at

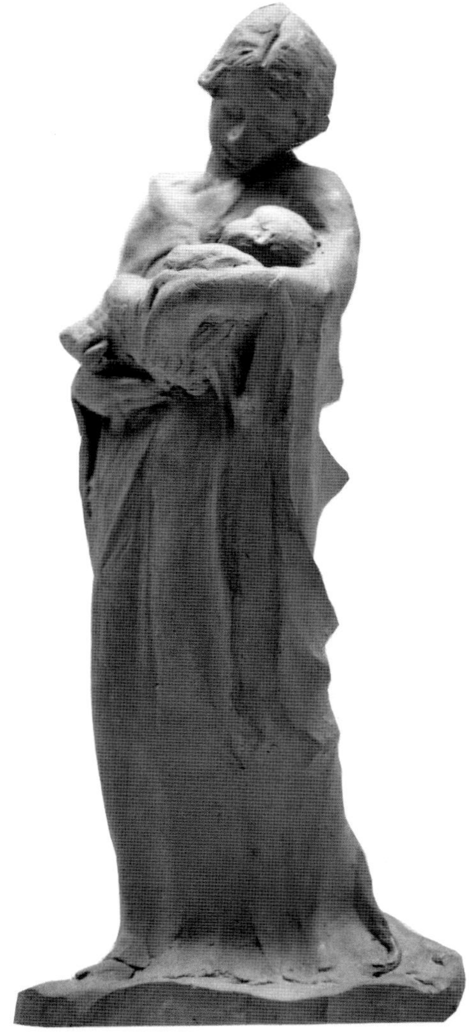

Cat 4. Mother and Child, 1873-79

South Kensington, Queen Victoria's daughter Princess Louise had set a royal precedent studying clay modelling at the government-run Art Training School.[12] In January 1873 Mary was admitted to 'The Slade', the new Fine-Art School in Gower Street where Edward Poynter was introducing French *atelier* practice.[13] In dynamic clay modelling demonstrations the naturalistic sculptor Aimée-Jules Dalou, a refugee from the Paris Commune, showed how sculpture came from the heart of the clay, rather than the surface.[14] Mary left The Slade to study privately with Dalou whose influence can be seen in the deep-cut drapery and tender facial expression of her early terracotta *Mother and Child* (Watts Gallery), worked, as it were, from within the clay.

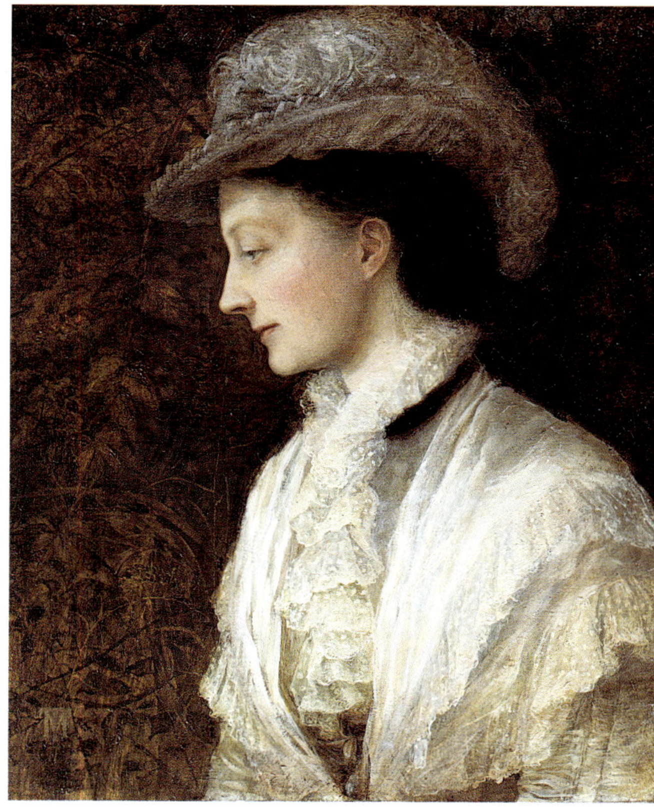

Cat 6. Etheldred Fraser Tytler, 1875

After Signor's new house at Freshwater, The Briary, was completed, he and Mary visited each other's studios. Both devotees of Ruskin, they would bemoan the stifling effect of the Machine Age on individual creative design and yearned for the revival of craftsmanship. In September 1875 he saw her portrait of *Ethel,* commissioned for Aldourie Castle. Its formal composition and her art training have resulted in a tighter discipline and less passionate paint handling than Christina's portrait of 1870.[15]

During a spellbinding interlude in March 1876, Mary's affections transferred to the mercurial Scottish Academician, George Paul Chalmers. An impassioned artist, he would veer from bubbling enthusiasm and elation when his art went well, to periods of doubt and depression. His poetic nature appealed to women, not least Mary. She felt his female portraits surpassed even Signor's. Chalmers painted her portrait in half a dozen sittings at his Edinburgh studio. So strong was her own passion for art that she would confuse mutual artistic ideals with love.

'I felt that extraordinary sensation, that some few pictures can give me; I remember most distinctly feeling it with Mason's.' [the Etruscan School painter, George Mason (1818-72)] 'It is a physical impression, as well as a mental one. I have known a feeling like it, after a meeting with one person (there is I suppose only one in the world for each, who could excite it) – I was exhausted – happy, out of myself. It is a curious mystery how strong the similarity is between Love and Art. I believe a picture must be specially poetical to have this influence. It is so for me certainly. I have never known a picture of Millais give it in me. Mr Chalmers has two exquisite first thoughts for pictures, they felt to me like songs of Keats or Shelley's.'[16]

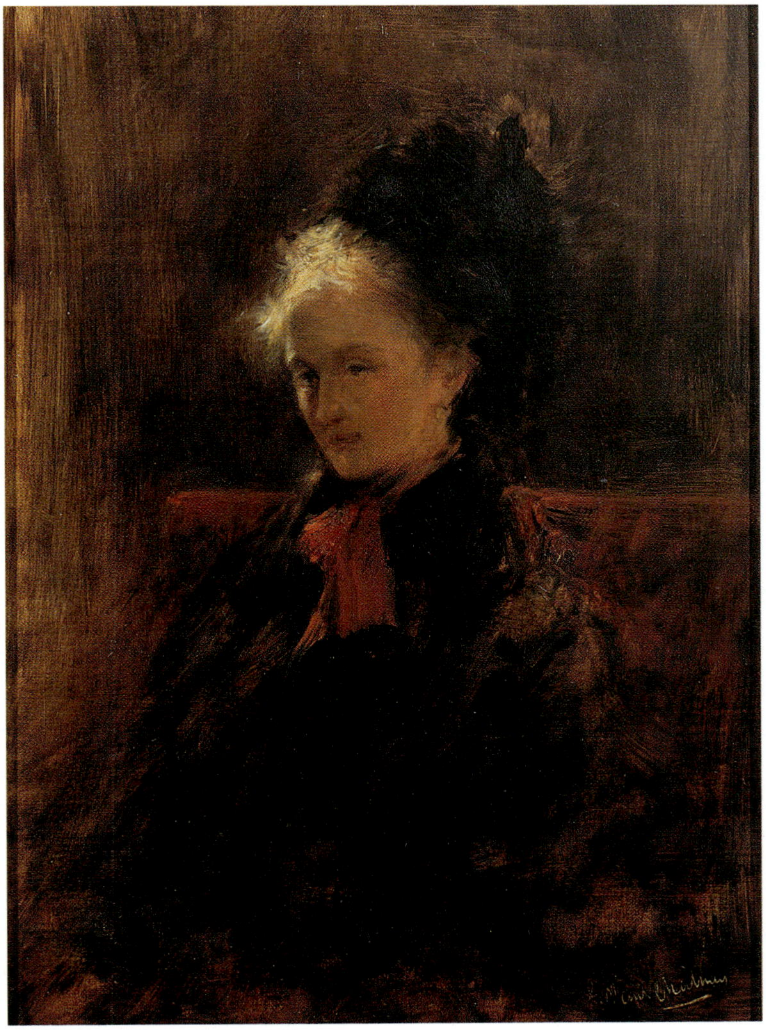

Cat 8. GEORGE PAUL CHALMERS, RSA

Mary Fraser Tytler, 1876

As far as male portraits were concerned Signor still reigned supreme. To compare them, Mary noted, was like comparing Titian and Van Dyck, whose influence is evident in her portrait of Ethel, but she was very much drawn to Venetian colour – 'Watts's influence no doubt – I feel in them a dignity and refinement and such colour as I can see in no other school.'[17] Chalmers left a lasting impression on her, but within two years, he was dead, murdered by thieves, or so the rumour ran.[18]

Mary's father died in January 1881 and she moved with her stepmother into 68 Eccleston Square, London. Dividing her time between London and her Sanquhar studio, Mary had become Signor's unofficial student, no mean position, for since his seminal *Love and Death* had been seen in the opening exhibition of the Grosvenor Gallery in 1877, there had been growing international interest in his pioneering imaginative work. Misunderstood and ridiculed for decades these paintings – later known as Symbolist – were heralded at last. Mary visited his one-man Grosvenor exhibition time and again in the winter of 1881-82. 'I have long perceived that whilst before some great master's pictures I feel wonder,' she wrote. 'Before yours I always feel *better*.'[19]

Mary's studio at Sanquhar

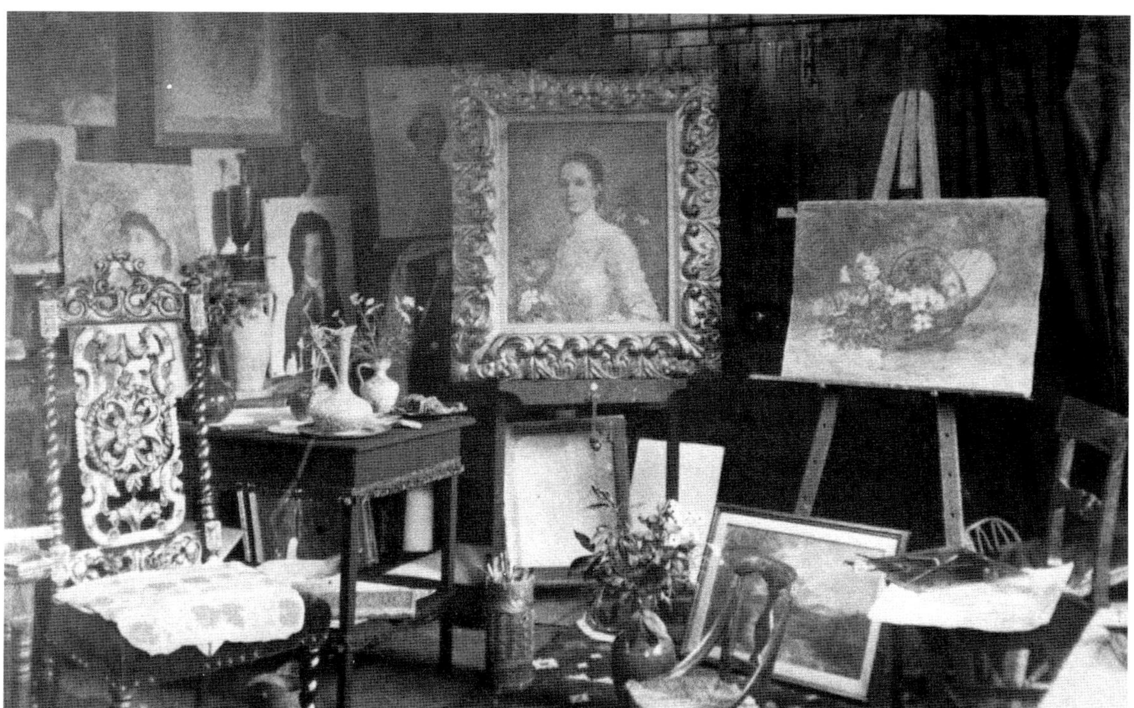

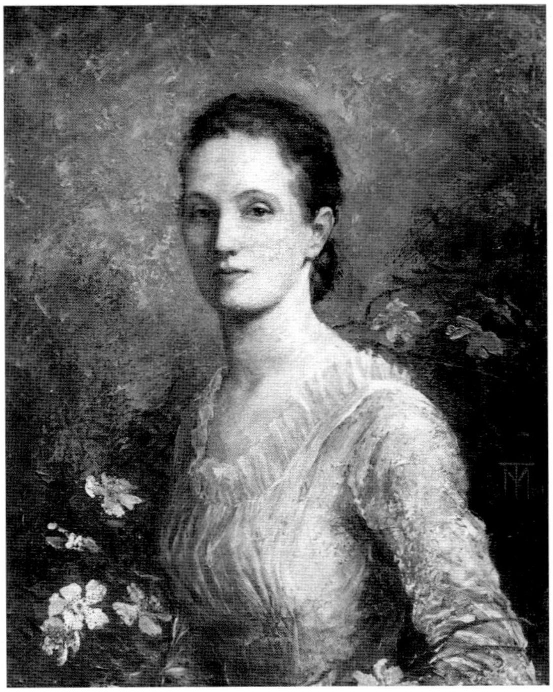

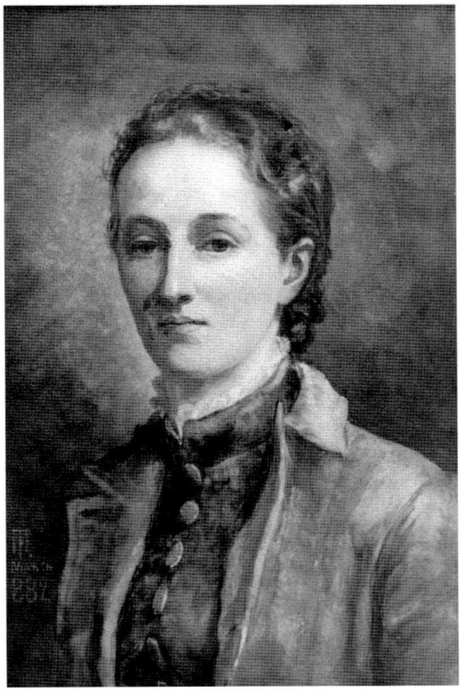

Self-Portraits,
Left: Cat 9, oil, 1881
Right: Cat 10, watercolour 1882

Mary studied from a portrait in his gallery at Little Holland House[20] in 1883 and began to see Signor in terms of more than a professional friendship. She announced with unaccustomed boldness, 'Signor, I think I have been looking for you all my life'.[21] Seeing their undoubted empathy in artistic and ideal thought as deeper love, she insisted in her letter of January 1885 that 'I grow when I am with you'.[22] He was pursuing a young American patron[23] at the time, and rebuffed Mary's advances.

'You are a silly Child, and confound a certain atmosphere in my studio arising from the intention of my work acting upon your artistic temperament with me the artist.'[24]

That winter she had embarked on a project that was to provide the springboard for the work of her life, enabling the poor to enrich their lives through craft training. Under the Reverend Barnett's scheme at St Jude's, Whitechapel,[25] Mary started a clay-modelling class for shoeblacks. Twice a week, she would leave her elegant Pimlico home to teach in the slums, a pioneer in an embryonic movement whose influence was to spread rapidly throughout the British Isles. In 1877, Eglantyne Jebb had started a woodcarving class for agricultural labourers and servants at Ellesmere in Shropshire. Her idea was to offer them a brighter life, to provide recreation and a counter-attraction to the public house through learning a craft that would equip them for a professional career.[26] Jebb's scheme – known first as the Cottage Arts Association, and encouraged by Charles Leland who had organized similar training in Philadelphia – burgeoned throughout the 1880s. Earl Brownlow was appointed President of the renamed Home Arts and Industries Association in November 1884[27] and the working classes throughout the country received instruction in woodcarving, brass repoussé, clay modelling, weaving and mosaic setting. Talented women, prevented from earning a living, trained as voluntary teachers – the Princess of Wales ran a woodcarving class. A central office and training studios were set up at Langham Place, and annual exhibitions of work produced in the Home Arts classes were held from July 1885. To Jebb, meeting Mary for the first time in 1886, was 'the chief event of my visit to town.'[28]

Signor, co-opted on to the Home Arts council by Lord Brownlow, sought support and designs from friends. Now playing a prominent part in the nationwide enterprise close to her heart, he wrote to her in March 1886, under the pretext of seeking advice about sending paintings to St Jude's – he had exhibited there for years.[29] On 3 July, fearing that she planned to marry one of her sitters, he told her, 'I want you'.[30]

At 36, Mary was more than three decades younger than 69-year-old Signor. Marriage to the influential Academician carried immense responsibility. She needed time to consider. Signor could not wait. A week later he wrote offering artistic reassurance and indicating that he hoped she would be able to assist him to fulfil his pledge to the nation – he was painting a portrait collection of nineteenth-century figures[31] and important Symbolist works planned originally as frescoes for his unfulfilled Michelangelesque House of Life.[32] His letter reveals, however, that Mary felt she would have to give up her own art – a supreme sacrifice – in order to help him.

'I did not intend to write to you again as it was agreed you were to sweep me away, at least for a time, but whether or no you will ever come to help me with my work, which after the things dedicated to the nation shall be finished, I wish to be devoted to charitable purposes, and whether or no you will be able to go on with your painting in the life that may be yours I am extremely regretful to think you are losing any chance of improvement. Later it may be possible to put you in communication with the teacher I spoke of, meantime you cannot do better than try to produce in the qualities of your watercolour drawings, purity of tone and precision of outline. I won't add more. Do not answer but always believe me to be yours.'[33]

Aldourie

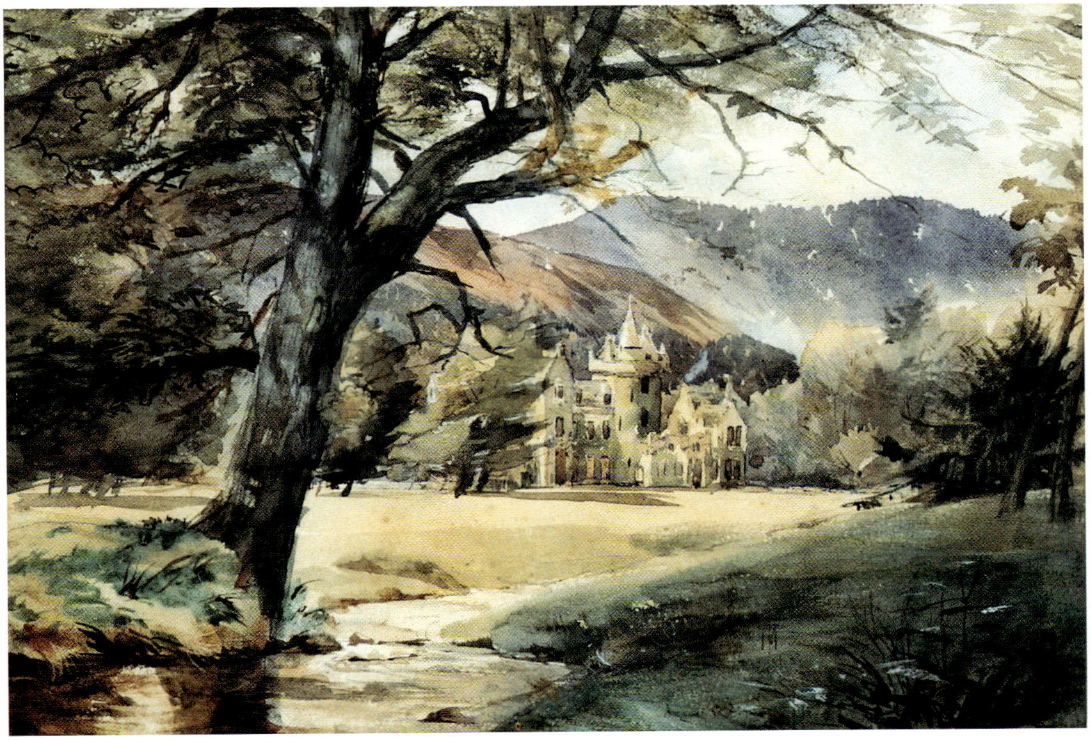

On 25 July 1886, Mary accepted.[34] Sixteen years after their first meeting, she had secured a partner in whose ideals she believed wholeheartedly and whom, at last, she could love. To share his artistic ideals and live amongst his noble works was no doubt a joy and a privilege. But it required courage to marry the man, with his distinguished circle of friends, beautiful admirers and – most demanding of all – his idiosyncratic genius. The women who flirted with him and worshipped his art – even Emilie Barrington, his predatory neighbour who had imposed herself as its guardian – were married and had never had to tie themselves entirely to him. At his easel, Signor's imagination – whether melancholy or enthusiastic – was directed on to canvas. But outside his studio, Signor, nervous and hypersensitive and unbusinesslike, suffered unpredictable crippling migraines. The stigma of his divorce remained. Mary's family, however, were delighted by her news – not to say intrigued. As her half-brother, William, put it, 'Let us know the day, and Ted and I will be there to give you to the Nation.'[35]

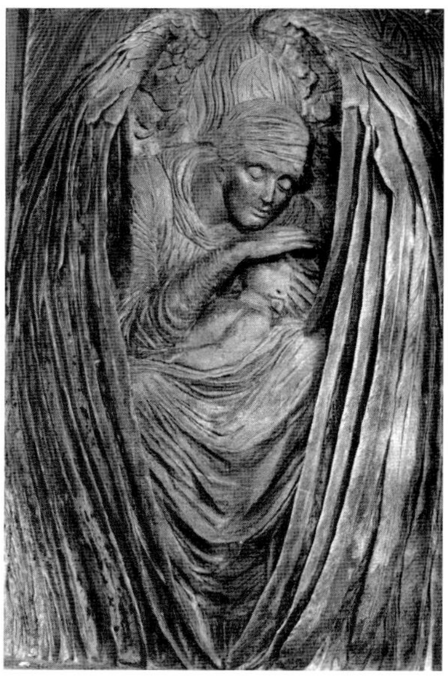

Death Crowning Innocence, bronze, 1891, after the painting by G F Watts

Six weeks before the event, on 7 October, her young nephew died following a fall from his horse. Signor sent his mother a chalk drawing of *Death the Angel Crowning Innocence*, as a design for a memorial showing the Angel of Death cradling a child. After their marriage Mary modelled it in clay and had it cast in bronze with her reliefs of his *Love and Death* and *The Messenger* to form a triptych at the entrance to the family cemetery at Aldourie.[36]

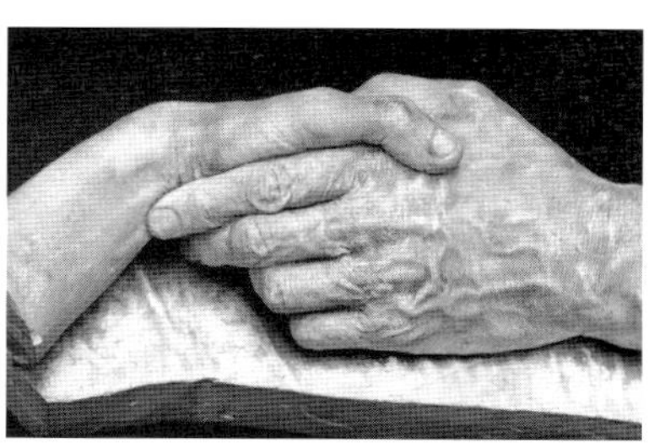

Cast of the left hands of Mary and Signor, 1889

Signor and Mary were married on Saturday 20 November at Christ Church, Epsom near her stepmother's home. Their six-month honeymoon was spent in Egypt and Greece, where he introduced her to 'the keynote to all that is beautiful in art.'[37] Fearing at first that 'his light might mean <u>blindness</u> to me',[38] she took heart from his teaching and his motto 'Forward and Fear Not'[39] and kept records of his thoughts in her journals. Until their marriage her chief focus had been easel painting. Now as they sailed down the Nile, she resolved to design decorative art to symbolize high ideals, Wattsian thought. Her flamboyant sketches of ships in full sail to symbolize 'Forward and Fear Not'[40] which were to ornament a mantelpiece at Little Holland House and of an Egyptian winged sun and curvilinear asp intended for their porch are the earliest example of the sinuous strength that would characterise her decorations on the Watts Chapel. A devotee of Ruskin, she observed that the shadow cast by a creeper on to their hotel wall in Cairo seemed finer than the plant itself – 'the flatness of the shadow made the decoration more perfect for that purpose than the real plant'[41] – its interwoven pattern, as it were, anticipating her Art Nouveau entrelac inside the chapel.

Signor painted an oil sketch of Mary in Pera, Turkey,[42] and the two Symbolists arrived back in Kensington on Saturday 4 June, shortly before the golden jubilee of Queen Victoria. 'And now the peaceful life in art began for me,' wrote Mary. While Signor exchanged news with Leighton, she sat in front of *Chaos* in Little Holland House Gallery, absorbing the spirituality of her husband's mind which seemed to glow from the canvas. 'Surely I shall assimilate something of its living soul with mine.'[43]

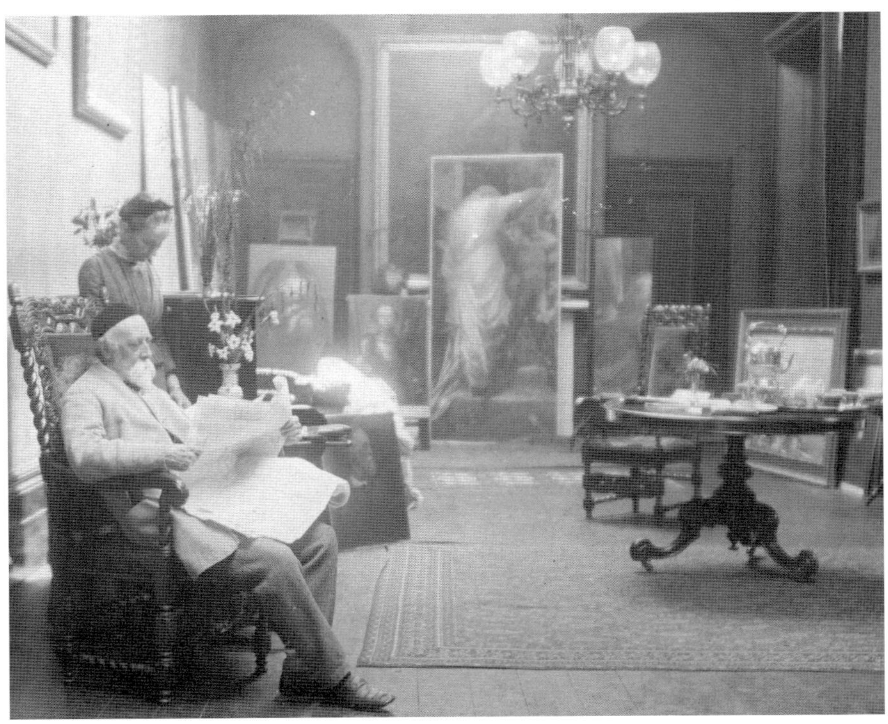

Mary and Signor at Little Holland House

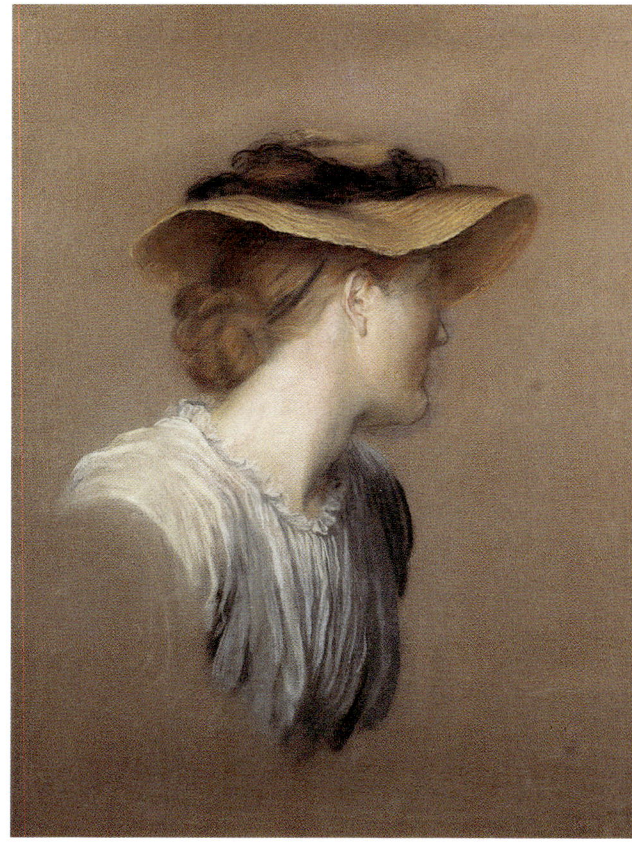

GEORGE FREDERIC WATTS

Portraits of Mary, 1887

Right: painted in Turkey

Below: at Little Holland House

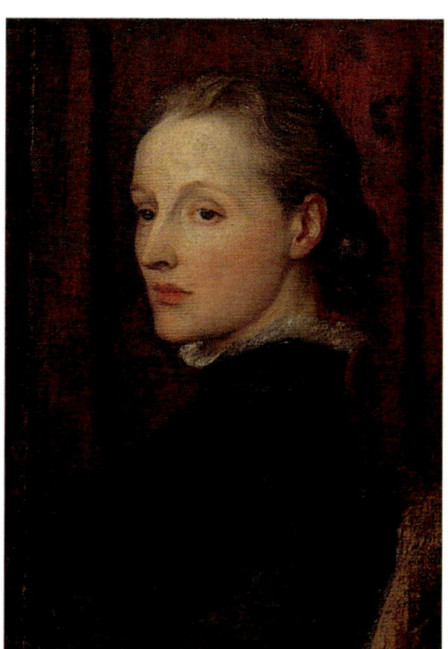

As his wife, Mary had access to leading craftsmen of the day. She discussed her plans for decorative art with Edward Burne-Jones, who sent Osmund Weeks, Walter Crane's assistant, to help her prepare *gesso duro*,[44] the popular Arts and Crafts medium. Manipulating the traditional fibrous plaster with gusto she covered Signor's new reading alcove – it was designed to focus the sound as the slightly deaf artist lay on his *chaise longue* – with gilded gesso decoration. Although no visual record remains, it was admired by Burne-Jones – 'how aggressively happy you looked that evening, lolling on velvet, and with a background of gold'[45] and Signor referred to its decoration as 'the first page of a beautiful book.'[46]

Mary worked in his old Iron House studio, tolerating his interruptions offering advice or summoning her to study special textural effects or the way fine, sharp lines achieved quiet and reticence. She studied musculature and bone structure with his former assistant, Henry Moore,[47] photography from W J Stillman[48] and Fred Hollyer,[49] and sat for two further portraits by her husband. Yet under his shadow she felt artistically frustrated, 'Instead of my work, I focus him. It will take me a little while yet to get over being under the shadow of his great work.'[50] She yearned to teach a Home Arts class. In the meantime she became, with Signor, a council member of the South London Fine Art Gallery, part of the free library founded by William Rossitter to educate the poor through art, and of the burgeoning Home Arts and Industries Association which had moved into headquarters at the Royal Albert Hall.

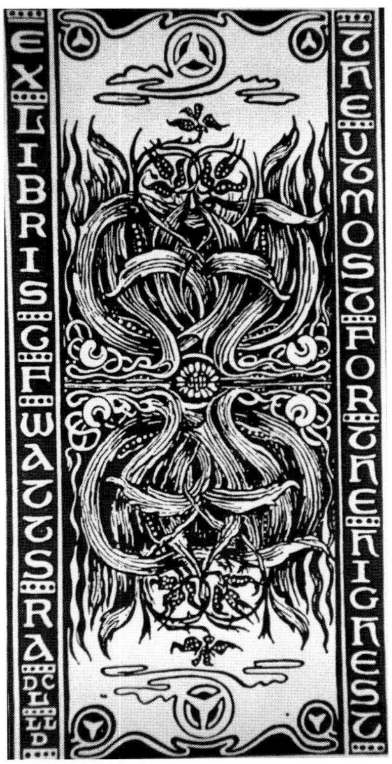

Signor's bookplate, 1888

Mary bought Signor a seal for use as a bookplate for Christmas 1888 and asked him to compose a motto for her to engrave upon it. 'The Utmost for the Highest', he replied. He was delighted by her idea for its decoration inspired by their Benvenuto Cellini's autobiography – 'a pool reflecting a star'. 'Oh yes! A little puddle, that will do beautifully for me.'[51]

The women's suffrage movement had been developing in Britain throughout her life. In May 1889, Sir Frederic Leighton, the President of the Royal Academy, wrote to Signor, his closest friend, to enlicit Mary's support for his sister's appeal in *The Nineteenth Century* against the proposal to extend Parliamentary suffrage to women.

'Now I want you to ask Mrs Mary something from me. There is at this moment a movement in contemplation in which many well-known women take an active interest – women like Mrs Lynn Linton, Lady Alwyn Compton, Mrs Humphrey Ward, Miss Beatrixe Potter, and which *opposes* itself to the attempt to obtain the *suffrage* for women – thereby drawing them out of the natural sphere in which they exercise such enormous and beneficial influence ... *Does the Signora sympathise with this view?* . . . if she is in sympathy could she, think you, enlist Lady Tennyson and Mrs Hallam Tennyson . . .'[52]

Quite the contrary, Mary, a keen suffragist, considered feminine influence beneficial to politics, and that women's suffrage was a just and natural development of educational reform. The President accepted her refusal with characteristic grace. 'I rather suspected later,' Mary commented, 'that Sir Frederic himself was but a lukewarm opponent.'[53]

A pivotal project into which she could at last channel her creative energy, began in early 1890, after Signor commissioned Ernest George to build the Watts house beside the Pilgrim's Way at Compton in Surrey. They named it 'Limnerslease' – 'Limner' to identify it as an artist's home and 'leasen' the Old English word meaning 'to glean, our hope being that there were *golden years* to be gleaned in this new home.'[54] Building started in April 1891 and Mary embarked on highly imaginative schemes to decorate it.

Symbolic gesso ceilings, an ever more flamboyant reading alcove, fire surrounds and bed ends were conceived and created according to Ruskinian principles widely disseminated through the *Hobby Horse* magazine, the National Association for the Advancement of Art and its Application to Industry and the Arts and Crafts Exhibition Society exhibitions. The A&CES had been set up by the Art-Workers' Guild, which re-established the artist craftsman, unity in art and design and better understanding between painters, sculptors, architects, designers and craftsmen. In its first exhibition at the New Gallery in 1888 were textiles by C F A Voysey, Kate Holiday and Morris & Company, tiles by William de Morgan, a room decoration by W R Lethaby, Home Arts displays and a range of designs by A H Mackmurdo and the Century Guild and C R Ashbee's Toynbee Hall School and Guild of Handicraft. Ashbee, who had arrived at Whitechapel shortly after Mary stopped her classes for shoeblacks, visited the Watts' a number of times in the 1890s. As Walter Crane, the A&CES president, had been keen to revive the use of gesso, there were gesso panels by Heywood Sumner, Charlotte Wylie, Conrad Dressler, Crane himself and a Broadwood piano decorated by Kate Faulkner.

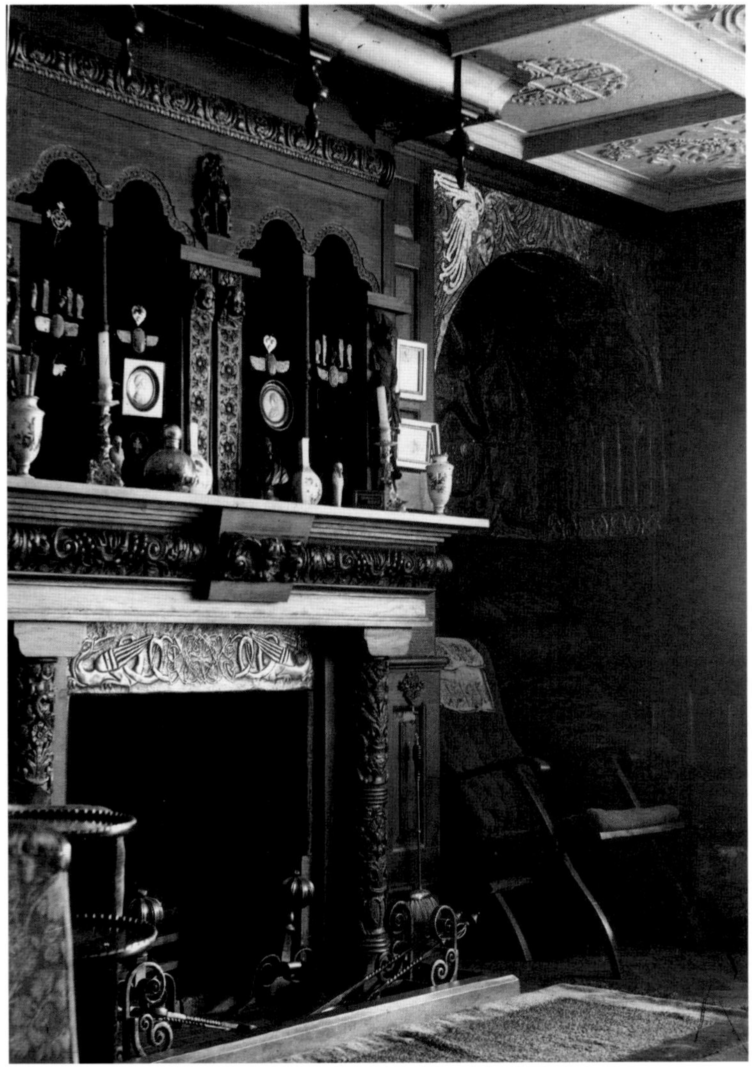

The Red Room, Limnerslease

Crane's paper in the catalogue[55] accorded with the Watts' creed that the three qualities essential to beautiful decoration were dignity and simplicity of line, harmonious colour and a suggestive idea. Furthermore, Patrick Geddes, writing in *Every Man His Own Critic*, the companion to the 1888 Glasgow International Exhibition, encapsulated the philosophy underlying Mary's Limnerslease schemes:

'as the poet may rise from the mere sensuous perfection of representment to the discernment of deeper meanings and higher harmonies, so . . . even more fully and profoundly) may and does the artist.'[56]

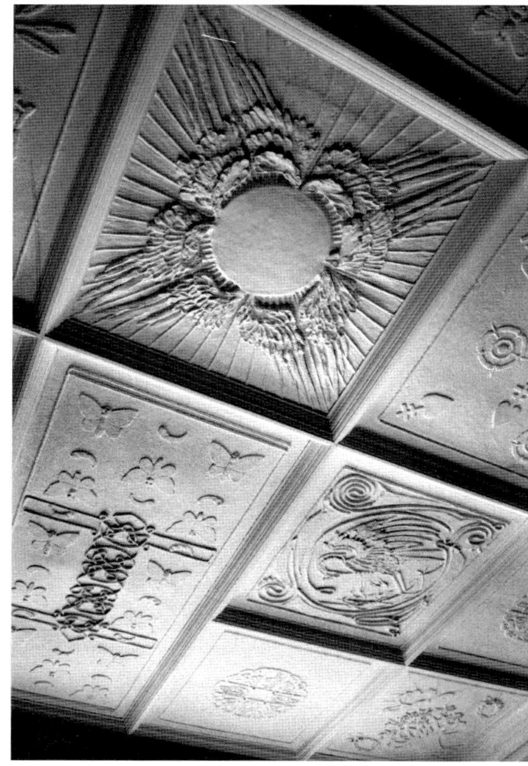

Right: The Red Room ceiling, showing the Winged Sun, Joy of the soul, Pelican, Olive Tree and the Blessing Hand. Below: Mary and assistant preparing gesso panel

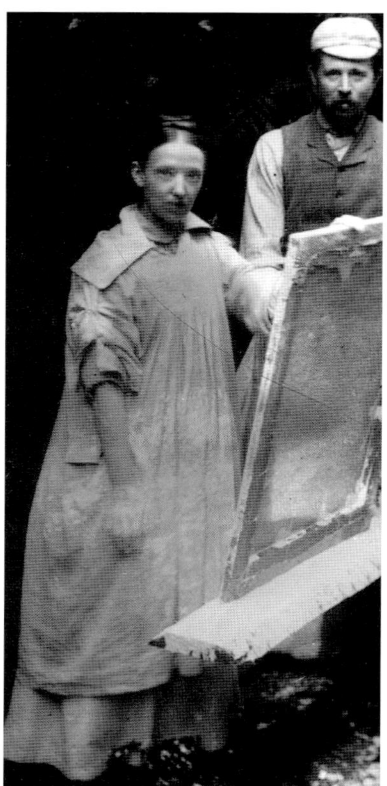

Mary's all-embracing plan for the Red Room ceiling at Limnerslease was to celebrate in panels of Early Christian, Egyptian and Celtic-inspired symbols, joys of the soul, the mind, sensibilities and senses. As her memorial to her husband, its decorative scheme was to be 'the concrete expression of the spiritual atmosphere that Signor has around him – the aroma of his thought put into the silent language of my symbols.'[57] Ruskin's *Queen of the Air* was her point of departure, and as in Celtic art, her symbols convey multiple meanings, although the motif looks simple. Powerful in thought suggestion, her panels of stylized stucco symbols were fairly coarsely modelled and all the more vibrant for it.

Radiating from the centre of the coffered ceiling her relief of the Winged Sun – with four pairs of wings and rays pointing to the corners of the earth – suggests 'The Heavens declare the Glory of God'. The sun itself evokes Life and the Universe, its circular shape, Eternity, Unity of the law of Creation and the wings suggest Loving Shelter, Spiritual Life and Motion, 'the primary law of all

Vitality.' In this central motif alone Mary appears to be embroidering Signor's theme *Love and Life*. Double panels stretching across the ceiling from the Winged Sun symbolize qualities towards which human life should aspire. Like squared Egyptian cartouches each incorporates her characteristic Celtic cross of hearts. There is a butterfly and chrysalis to symbolize faith in after-life, a bee and cell (work), the heart, double cross and rose (goodness, sacrifice) – roses representing incorruptibility to Christians and faithfulness to Greeks – vines and corn (peace and plenty). Interspersing these were daisy-shaped panels of the Blessing Hand. Intended to evoke Signor's dictum 'Remember the Daisies of Life' – to take utmost care over small details – the segments comprise a crowned heart interwoven with palms of Peace and within the arms of a cross is God's Blessing Hand.

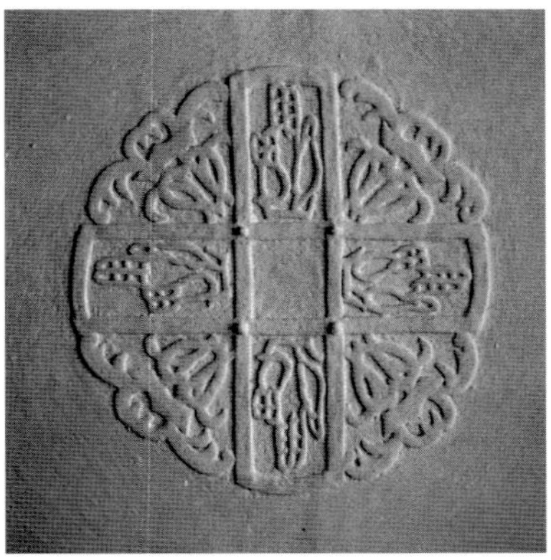

The Blessing Hand

Lettering and the Celtic cord – interweaving, spiralling motifs – are material to her 'painter's window' above the bay window which she devoted personally to Signor. It was completed five years later, in 1896,[58] by which time Mary had studied Celtic manuscripts, and her style had become more fluid – even flamboyant. The patterns are predominantly Celtic in inspiration, laced with a touch of Art Nouveau. Based on her design for *The Utmost for the Highest*, the main feature is an exotic pattern of stars and intertwining plant-life reflected in a pool. Side panels refer to a ninth-century Anglo-Saxon manuscript design of a peacock – sacred to Brahmins and Buddhists; its coiled neck and beak are interlaced with Celtic knots in the form of hearts and the cord supporting Buddhist medallions indicate *Rita*, the right path. Finally, the swirling end panels celebrate Signor's birth and artistic life and work, with the sun setting amongst the sheaves of corn at Limnerslease.

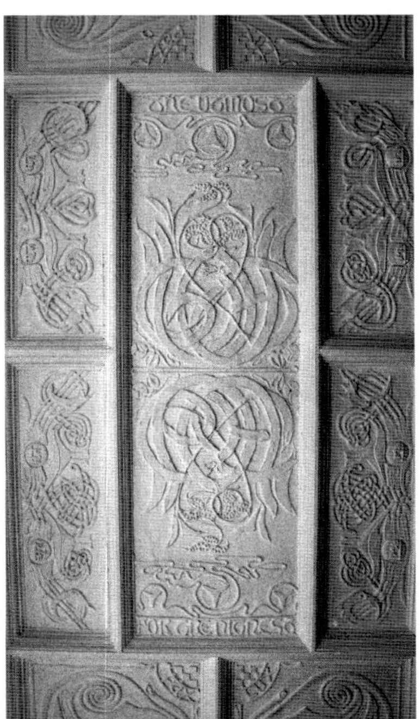

Signor's ceiling panels

As Mary modelled the creamy plaster, she recalled her governess's prophetic dream that she was her doing beautiful work which looked like carved ivory. At last, she thought, 'I am doing what I purposed to do at the beginning of my life with Signor and it makes it the most delightful work I have ever done.'[59] When her husband asked her into the studio to talk to Walter Crane – she was often called in to engage sitters in conversation at the start of a portrait – she took full advantage of the opportunity to seek the craftsman's advice. He informed that her fibrous plaster was not 'gesso' which was applied with a brush – she used her hands – but 'stucco'. Mary was appalled. '"Stucco" has such a hideous sound to one's modern ears, I am not inclined to be correct.' Crane's portrait, however, distressed her more because Signor had achieved a rare 'forward look', but had lost the effect the following day.

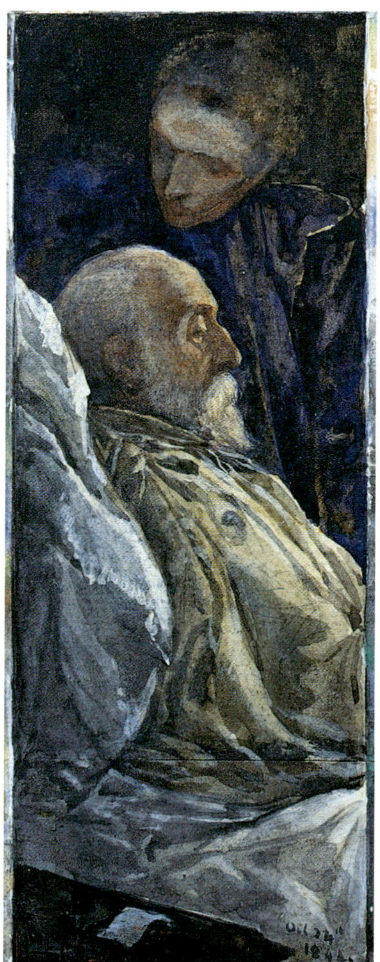

Cat 27. Signor, October 1894

'The sorrows of the artist's wife are upon me. Yesterday Walter Crane's portrait was entrancing, an epitome of his life, that really [is] a work of genius, today Signor had it in worked of it – the glory of it is dead! the soul has gone out like a light – It is nothing more than an ordinary portrait. Will it ever come again?'

Mary persuaded her husband to strengthen the chin, yet still she was unsatisfied and insisted he should make a further attempt to retrieve the look, for 'a breath makes or unmakes the spirit in a face'. Crane returned, and the portrait improved. Although Mary felt the earlier magic was never quite recaptured[60] to Millais the portrait was 'sublime'.[61]

Her own fantastic design for Signor's reading alcove at Limnerslease (1893) no longer exists, but photographs remain. It was a triumphant work. Because of the complex ceiling, she noted that it should not be 'over elaborate', but 'simple and great in idea and design'. Wrestling with her fertile, multi-facetted, spiritual imagination, she picked out apposite strands for an illuminated masterpiece, effectively their *Last Judgment*, to fill the six-foot arch.[62] Epitomising the design philosophy of Lethaby, it was covered in the bold Celtic-style decoration that would foreshadow the glorious interior of the Watts Chapel.

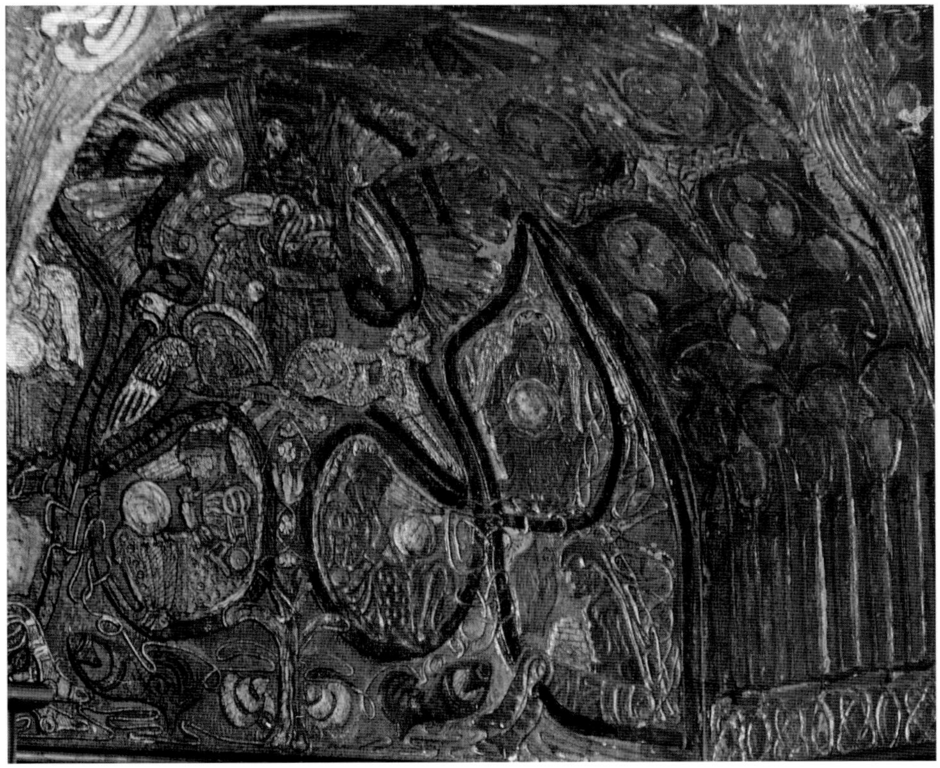

Signor's reading alcove, Limnerslease, 1893

'The Celtic seems in character the most decorative symbolic style there is,' Mary recorded in her journal. 'You have men women angels beasts and birds all twisted and knotted in with pattern, an integral part of it. The fault of the Celtic is that it is *unrestful*, "too busy" Mr George would call it. It is the fault of much Indian and Arabic work. Walter Crane advises the decorator to put away *all* styles from his mind and look at nature and trust to his own invention. Signor agrees with me that it should be an outgrowth of some style particularly sympathetic for the expression of one's idea. Walter Crane's decoration is very pictorial and it is fairly easy to decorate in that style, but to tie yourself to *pattern making* which is my ideal – though I can't reach it – is much more difficult.'[63]

Rising to the challenge, Mary studied the facsimile of the *Book of Kells* and Celtic objects at the British Museum. Her drawings and tracings were livelier, more *mouvementé* than the original designs, which, according to Arts and Crafts ethic, served as points of reference and inspiration rather than imitation. She explained to Signor that her scheme would express their whole range of thought. Interwoven into her patterns would be flowers, trees, birds, beasts, man and his double nature – spirit and flesh – the sun, stars, moon, angels, and a great light from which they would veil their faces; papyrus and poppies would appear as symbols for books and rest. Finally, added this indomitable woman, she wished to incorporate poetry, art, science, religion, history and fiction. Her husband laughed.[64] Hadn't she vowed it would not be over elaborate?

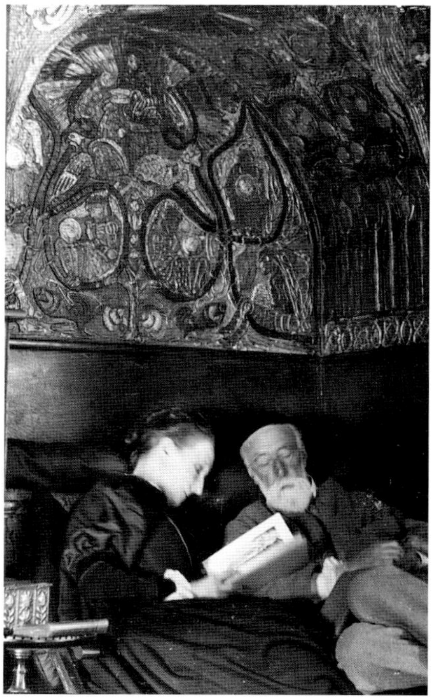

Mary reading to Signor at Limnerslease

In an astonishing tour de force, every creature, saint, knot and spiral, painted in glorious shades of crimson, blue, silver and old gold tempera was, of course, symbolic. Voluptuous-winged spirits filled the spandrels and the narrow arched soffit became the Firmament of Heaven, covered with symbols of the earth, moon and planets and the sun, its rays, as it were, illuminating the couple as they read.[65] A dynamic mélange of interlaced Celtic forms, Renaissance knights and even an interpretation of Signor's *All-Pervading*, the gesso decoration had been applied on to perforated zinc sheets and painted in tempera over white metal leaf which shone through the paint surface, giving an enamel-like lustre. So haunting was the imagery, however, that after Mary's death, Lily Chapman – the Watts' ward who came to live with them in about 1894 – had it destroyed.[66] But she left in place the brass repoussé fireplace.

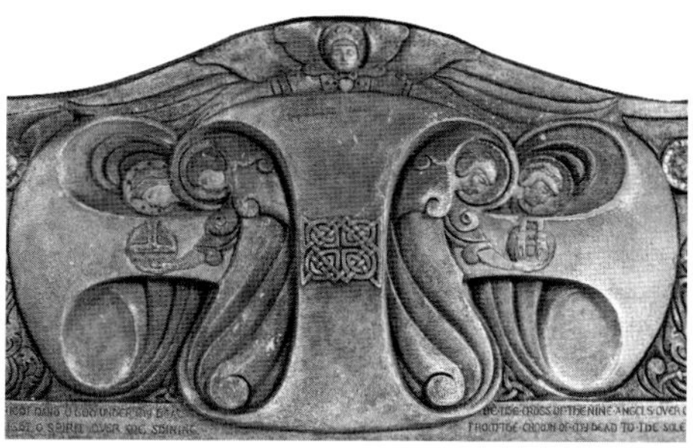

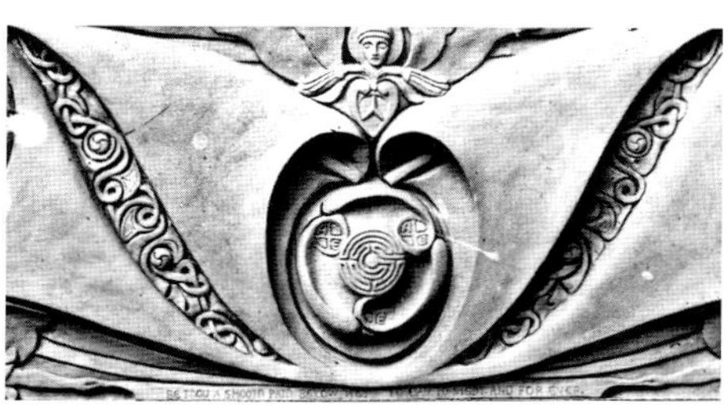

Above: Bedhead, 1901, detail
Below: Footboard, 1901, detail

Mary's scheme for the brass Red Room fire surround was based on the Prometheus myth. Recalling the Italianate high-relief decoration on gold ground upon which she had worked as a student at South Kensington – and surely also inspired by Crane's friezes – she tested her designs using gold paper. Signor was painting *Acis and Galatea* at the time. 'How delightful it is to work together in this way!' he exclaimed.[67] Now in February 1893 she covered the blazing, wilting gold paper with red and gold gauze, which allowed the pattern to show through, blending the whole together with a coppery shade, in preparation for the brass itself.[68] Presumably the fire surround was completed that year – if not by Mary herself, by a co-worker for the Home Arts and Industries Association.

Its three rectangular panels were to represent Unity, Peace and Loyalty. Across the top of the fireplace, which was to symbolize Unity – through the use of the Celtic cord – Mary turned the ninth-century peacock of her 'painter's window' into an eagle. Against a background coarsely beaten to represent the texture of rock, her repoussé design shows the eagle linked by elaborate interlace to Prometheus' chains and the central Celtic knot of hearts, woven into the form of a cross, symbolizing Redeeming Love.[69] Roses and columbines on the side panels represented Loyalty and Peace. Her Celtic cross of hearts appearing here in brass, and later in painted terracotta bedheads, in terracotta and gesso on the Watts Chapel and woven into a Donegal rug, became one of her favourite motifs.

High-relief carved mantelpieces and the vast intricate carved screen separating the drawing-room from the entrance hall, mirrors, copper trays and a range of objects at Limnerslease were carved or beaten out by Home Arts craftsmen and -women. The overall effect was reported by the *Westminster Budget*.

'The oak front door opens, and for a moment you stand quite dazzled in the brightness of a long, beautiful room. Black oak, catching gleams of light in its fantastic carvings, forms the background, and against it in an almost overwhelming variety of exquisite colours are so cunningly arranged that, notwithstanding this wealth of tints and shades, you have the impression of a perfect, subdued, harmonious *tout ensemble*, with only here and there a gleam of red copper, of yellow brass, of shimmering tinted glass. Over Mr Watts's special corner the arched roof is a mass of gilded colour ...'[70]

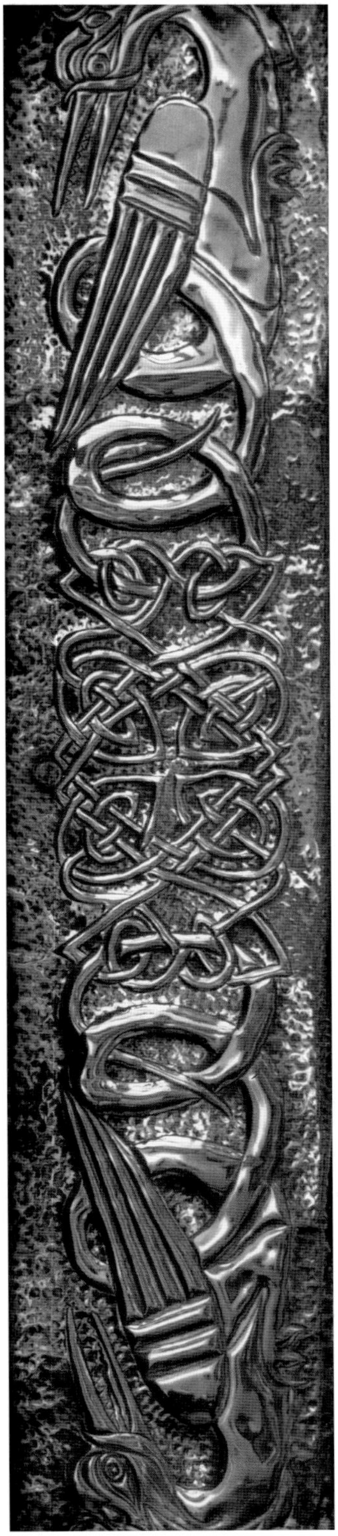

Prometheus in chains with Celtic cross of hearts on brass fire surround at Limnerslease, 1891-93

Opposite: *Cat 30. Watts Studio Fireplace; G F WATTS: Love Triumphant, Love and Death, Love and Life*

To Anny Thackeray Ritchie, describing the reading alcove in her journal in March 1896 as 'a sort of allegory of the sea and the earth and fullness thereof, and then the rays of light leading up to heaven', everything at Limnerslease seemed 'fragrant, kind, suggestive, the ceilings meant one thing, the walls another. I listened and seemed to be refreshed redipped in the waters of life – and hope.' 'It is all her doing,' Signor told Anny. 'She has a gift for it.'[71]

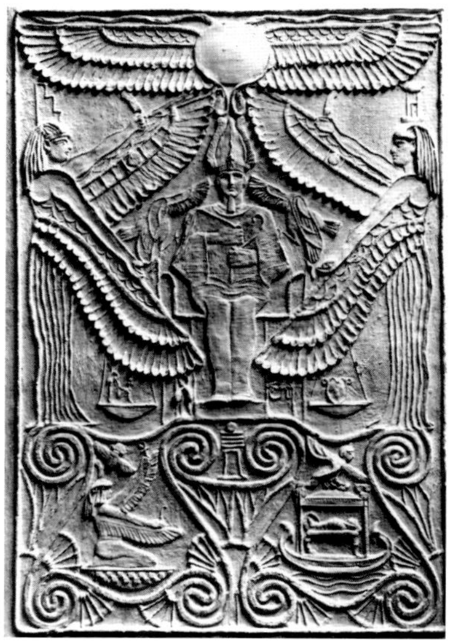

Mary's imaginative schemes in gesso and terracotta bas-relief were informed by extensive research into ancient religions and civilizations, for a second gesso ceiling scheme at Limnerslease was to have included twelve panels representing Egypt, Judaism, Brahminism, Buddhism, Assyria, and Christianity, Persia, Scandinavia, Rome, Greece, China and Central America. In the event only the first five were completed.[72] In the centre are three solar crosses taken from a Mississippi shell and gold discs found at Ballyshannon and in Assyria, their equilateral arms a Chinese symbol representing the earth. Despite the wide international range of thought and style, there is harmony in Mary's overall primitive Celtic stylization.

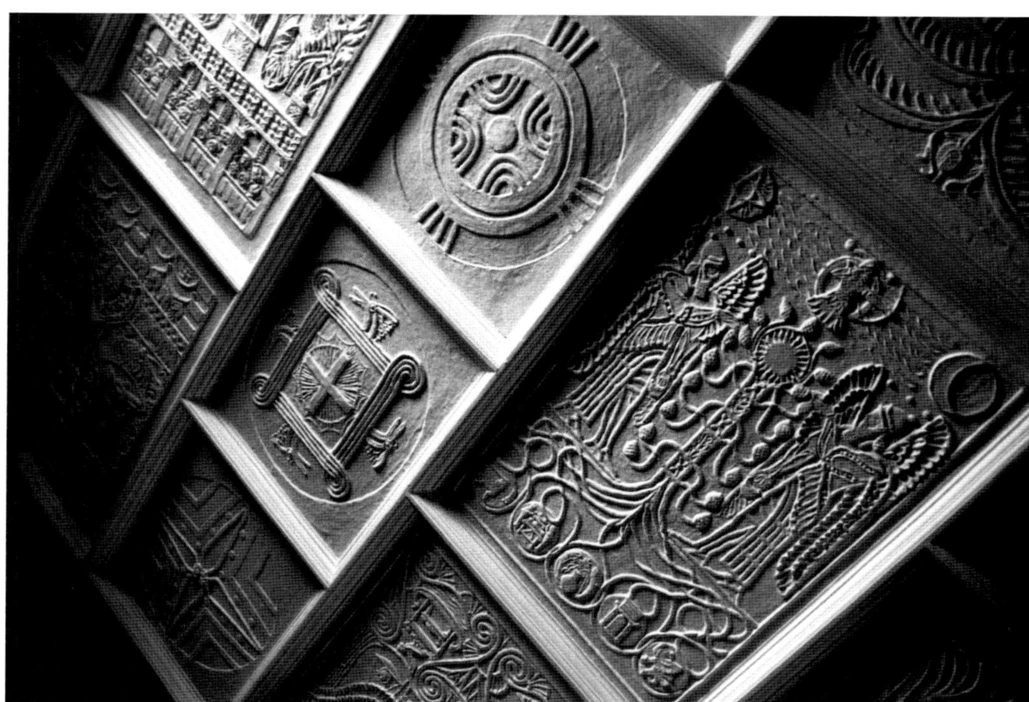

Above: Egyptian panel
Right: Ceiling of ancient civilizations

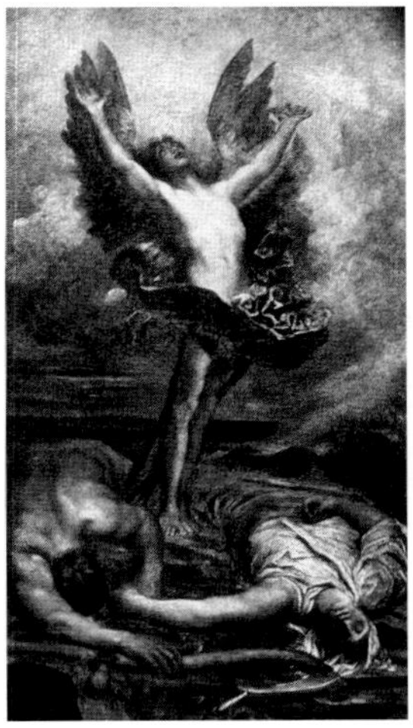

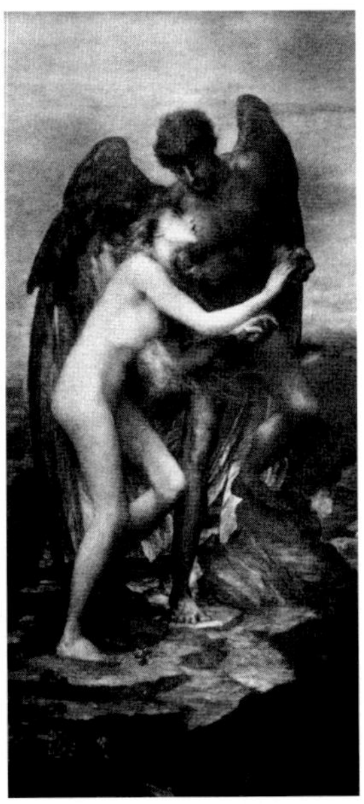

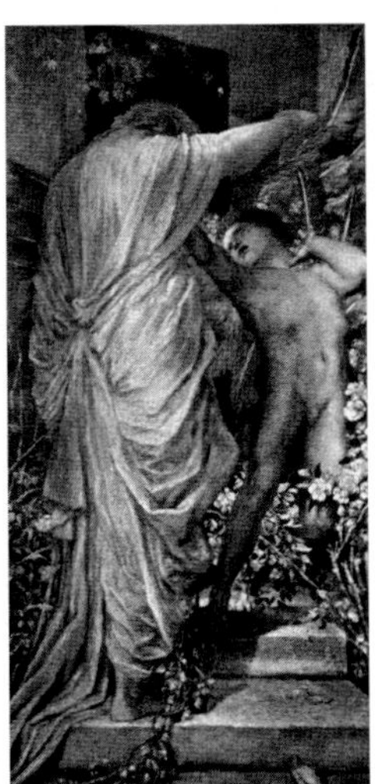

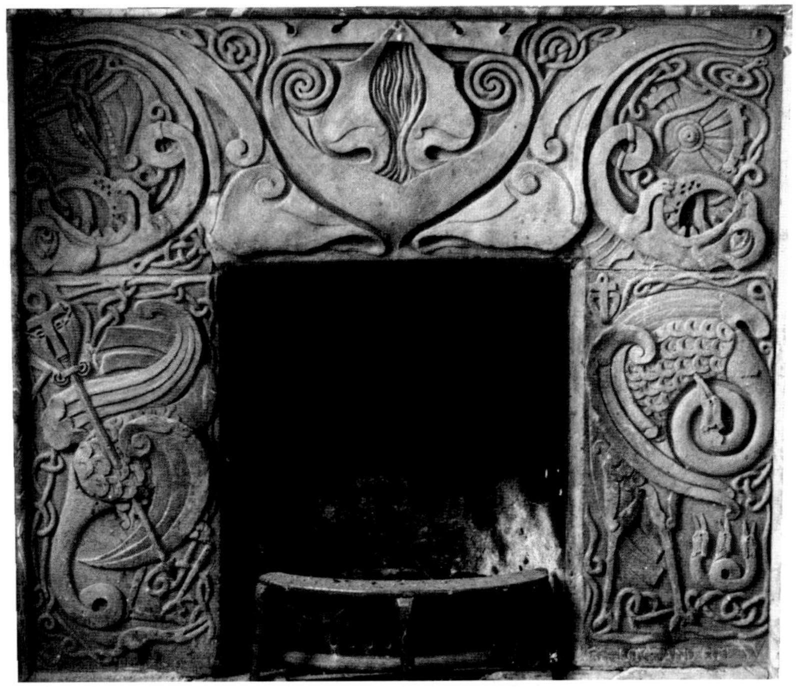

A dynamic example of Mary's eclectic expression of Wattsian themes is Signor's studio fireplace at Limnerslease, (1901), voluptuous Art Nouveau, Celtic-style interpretations in three terracotta panels – *Love and Death* and *Love and Life* surmounted by *Love Triumphant.* In his *Love and Death*, the huge robed personification of Death approaching a house which Love, a tragic youth with broken wings, attempts to shield. Her bas-relief shows an exotic winged pelican of Love pierced to death by a sword surmounted by a Viking mask with the Key of Life, the Egyptian symbol of Immortality. *Love and Life*, his tender painting of a winged figure of Love guiding the fragile female nude Life figure up the rocky path, was transformed by Mary into a winged pelican with a scrolled neck – presumably inspired by *The Medieval Bestiary* – pecking its flesh to feed the young chicks. Finally, in Signor's *Love Triumphant*, Love spread its wings over the falling personification of Time and the sleeping figure of Death; and in her relief stretching across the top of the fireplace, a central crowned scrolling heart triumphs over falling Anglo-Scandinavian creatures with jagged teeth and curling tails, representing Time (identified by a Brahman wheel) and Death (broken Cup of Life).

In the summer of 1893 Conrad Dressler told Mary of his plans to set up a medieval-style guild, a community of artists, training apprentices to make ceramic decorations in the style of Luca della Robbia (the Della Robbia Pottery at Birkenhead 1893-1906). Moved by his enterprise, Mary noted in her journal, 'Our workmen are hungry for this!'[73] She had designed the Marchioness of Waterford's memorial cross at Ford in 1891 – a joint project with Signor who had sent a design for the kneeling angels[74] – and was seriously thinking of starting a Home Arts class to teach memorial design[75] when the very opportunity presented itself in Compton. The parish council announced plans to purchase a plot of land near Limnerslease at Budburrow Hill for a new burial ground. 'My mind full of improving churchyards, memorials!' reads a brief journal entry on 4 September 1894. (Parts of her journals – these largely concern Signor – were unfortunately destroyed.) Five days later, she wrote, using her favourite Hindu expression, 'My hope is that Terra Cotta shall be my *Rita*.'

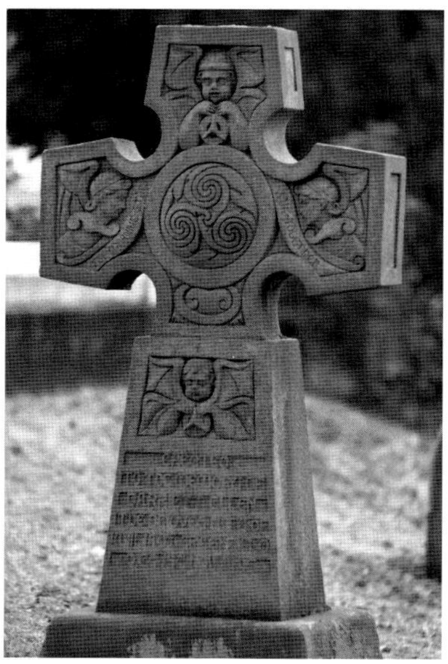

Memorial, 1895

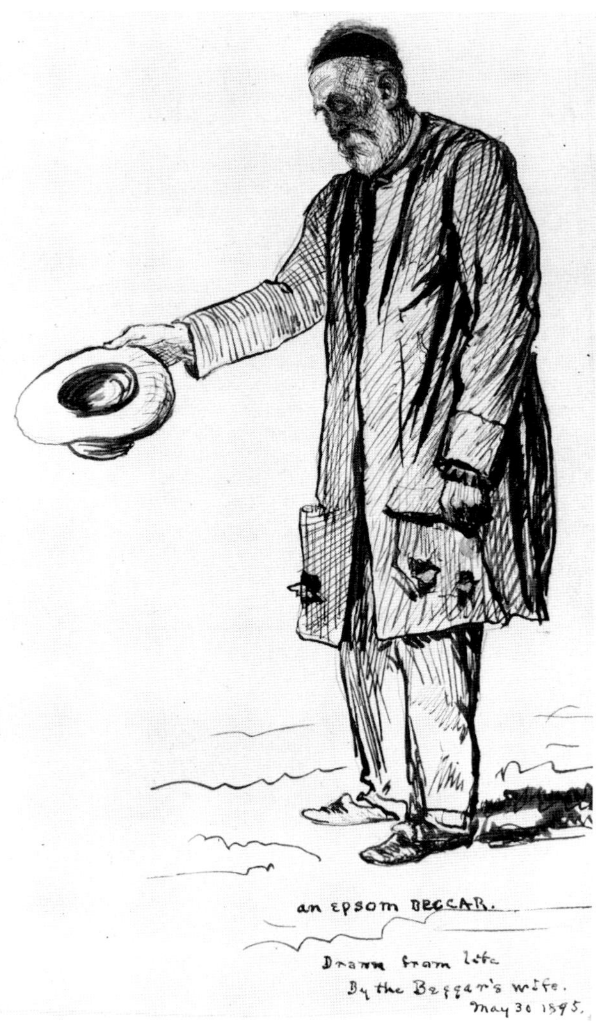

Cat 36. 'An Epsom Drawn from Life by the Beggar's Wife' – Signor begging for the Home Arts, 1895

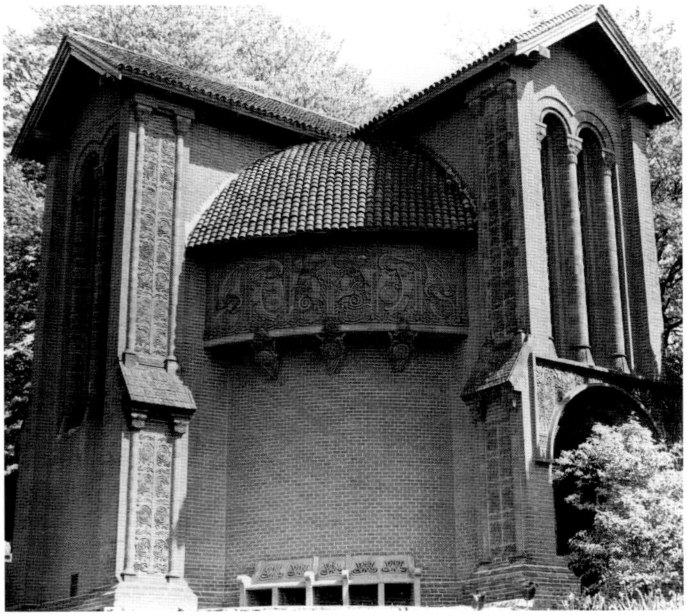

The Watts Chapel

The idea of a mortuary chapel followed – to be designed by Mary, built from local clay, modelled under her instruction at Limnerslease by local villagers, financed by portrait commissions painted by her long-suffering husband, and presented as a gift to Compton. For its pantheistic symbolism she drew on her research for the ancient civilizations ceiling and extended her Celtic style, infusing exotic patterns with the modern language of Art Nouveau. 'Decoration,' she wrote, 'must be *beautiful.* To be completely beautiful – it should be dignified & simple in line & harmonious in colour – & suggestive in idea.'[76]

Every structural detail of the mortuary chapel, from its circular cruciform shape to the buttresses, pillars, door, vaults and corbels exudes symbolic meaning.[77] Mary wrote in *The Word in the Pattern* that 'the patterns can claim to be more than are the letters of a great word: hieroglyphs'.[78] Yet their very exuberance almost rivals the 'idea'. For example, whereas her husband's famous picture of *Hope* shows a single figure seated on the globe playing the one remaining string of her lyre, Mary's terracotta Spirit of Hope panel on the 'Path of the Just'[79] frieze encircling the chapel is an intricate tapestry of winged spirits, peacocks and Celtic knots.

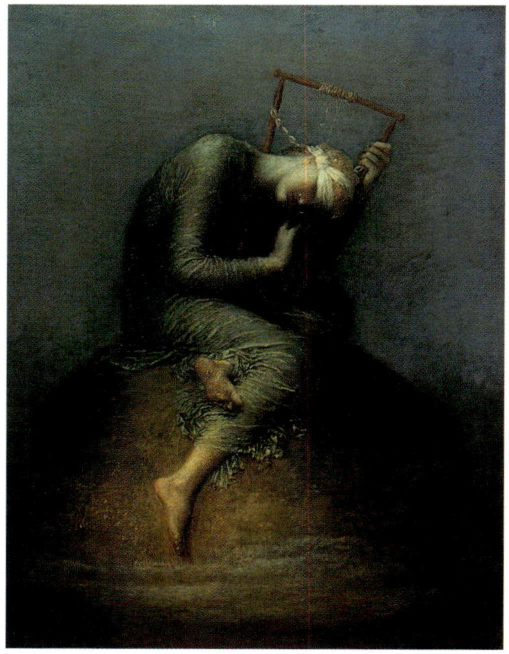

Angels with faces modelled in the manner of Rossetti and Burne-Jones – some in higher relief, suggesting Repose – and wings more curvilinear than Celtic representations, embrace roundels of birds and animals; the dove symbolizes Comfort, the hart, Aim or Aspiration, the lion suggests Courage and the spider, Patience. Beneath the double-armed cross and anchor, the peacock stands on a double Celtic cord whose knots were perhaps inspired by a border pattern on a carpet-page (abstract patterns) in *The Book of Durrow* (c675).[80]

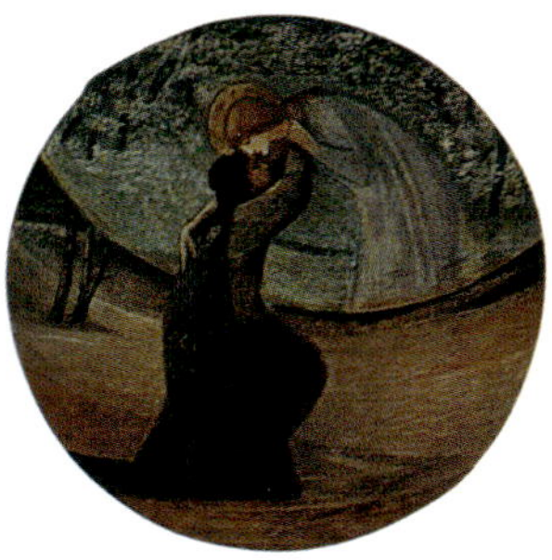

Above: G F WATTS, Hope, 1886
Left: Cat 51. SIR EDWARD COLEY BURNE-JONES, Golden Greeting, 1904
Below: Spirit of Hope frieze on the Watts Chapel, 1896-98

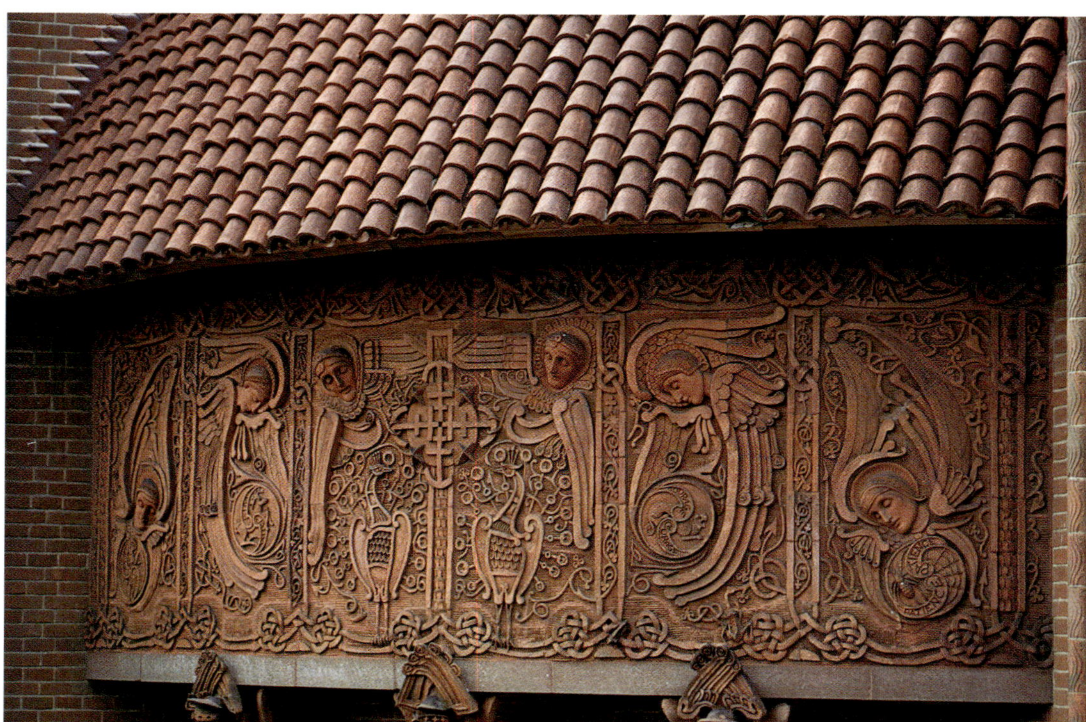

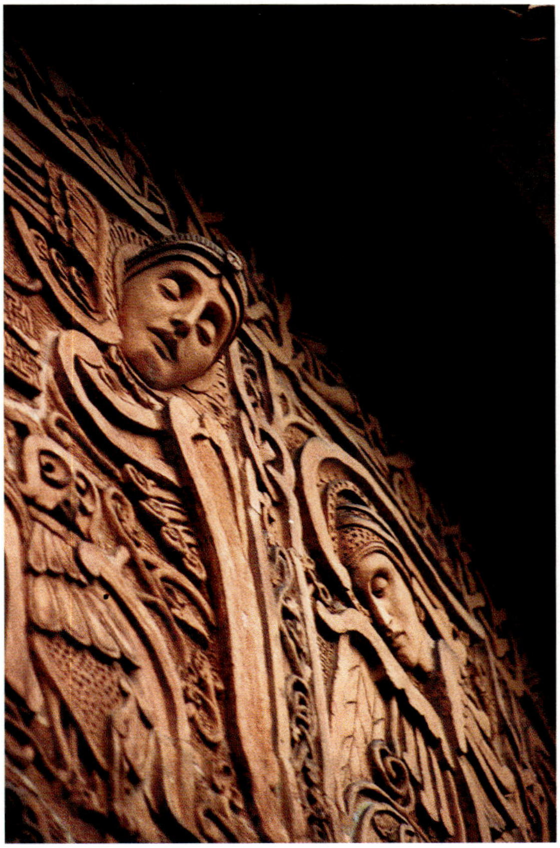

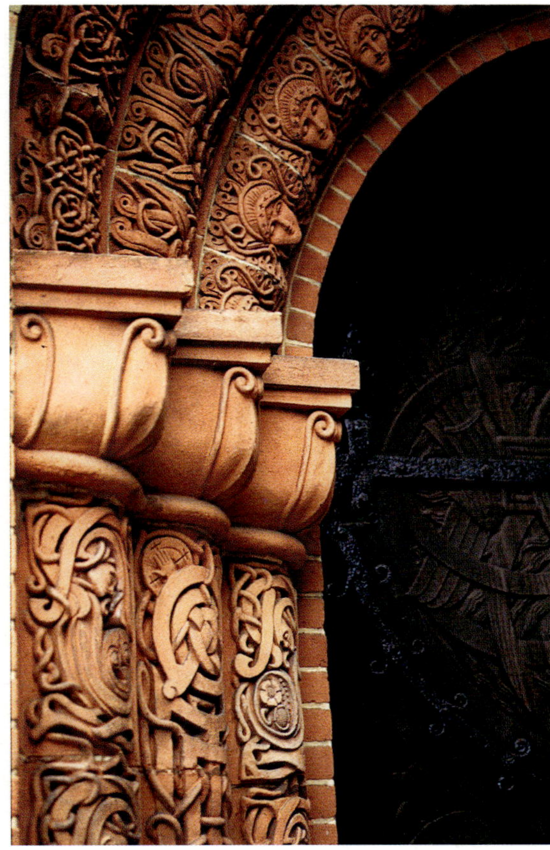

Above: Spirit of Truth, detail
Right: Chapel doorway, detail
Below: Boat of the Sun corbel, symbolizing the Truth and the Breath of Life

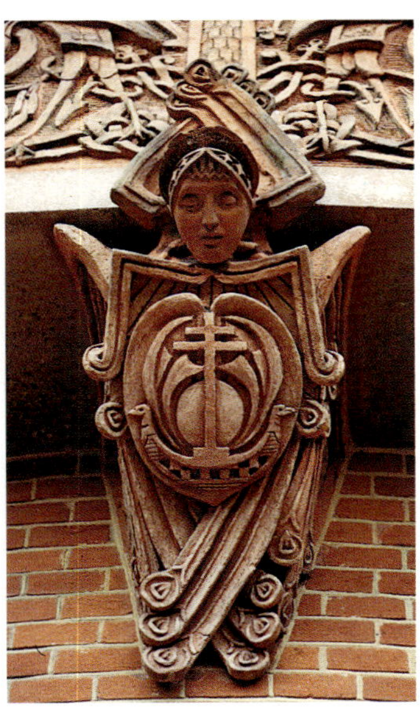

Bas-relief decoration carved on the chestnut casing of the oak door represents Man's Destiny, rising from an evil writhing dragon to a cross interlaced with wings and flames symbolizing Eternity, Light, Motion, Spirituality and Protection, above the Mystery of Darkness. The reeded cross was inspired by a wattle design carved on a gravestone in Iona and 'purified' – as Mary put it – back into wood; and the wrought iron hinges designed for her by the architect George Redmayne and made by the village blacksmith incorporate sails to symbolize the Breath of Life, with a T-shaped mast of the Tau cross.[81]

Six months after the villagers began to learn how to model clay, Mary took her Terra Cotta Home Arts class to the Royal Albert Hall to exhibit the chapel tiles at the 1895 Home Arts and Industries Association exhibition. *The Studio* highlighted their 'admirable capitals and surface fillings of modelled terra-cotta in rough clay baked in charcoal ovens to a most beautiful red.'[82]

By 1898 the mortuary chapel was built, its external decoration and curvilinear Art Nouveau seats were complete. But before embarking on the interior – and fervently against her husband's wishes – Mary decided to turn professional, to establish her own medieval-style guild to produce terracotta memorials, sundials, and garden ornaments. Installing young apprentices in a specially built hostel at the bottom of their garden in Compton – part of the Gallery (1903) she was having built for Signor by the Arts and Crafts architect Christopher Turnor – she set up Potters' Arts Guilds there and at Aldourie.

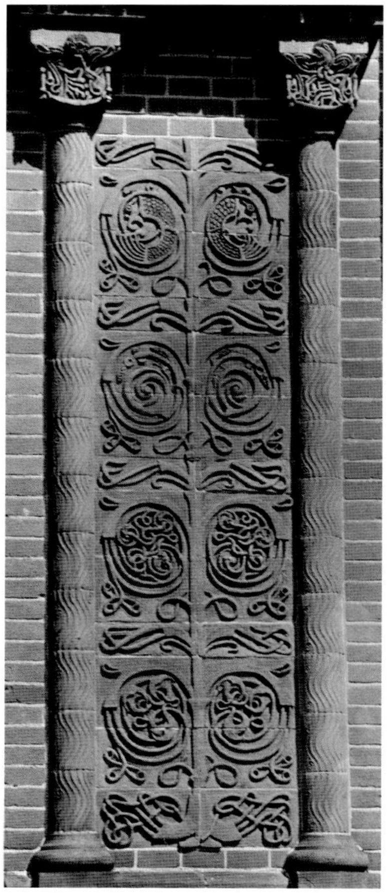

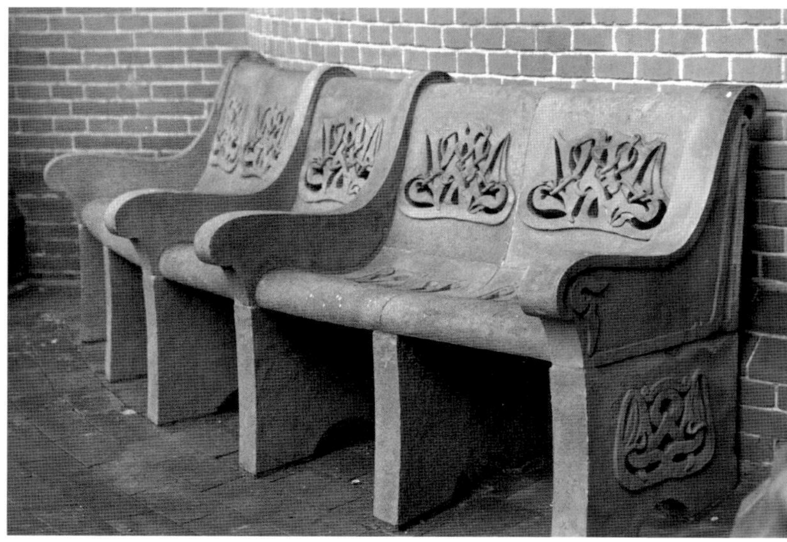

Above: Ripples of the River Of Life beside the spiralling Branches of the Tree of Life
Top right: Seats outside the Watts Chapel
Right: Memorial to Mary's sister Eleanor Kellie Maccallum Dalgleish, 1909

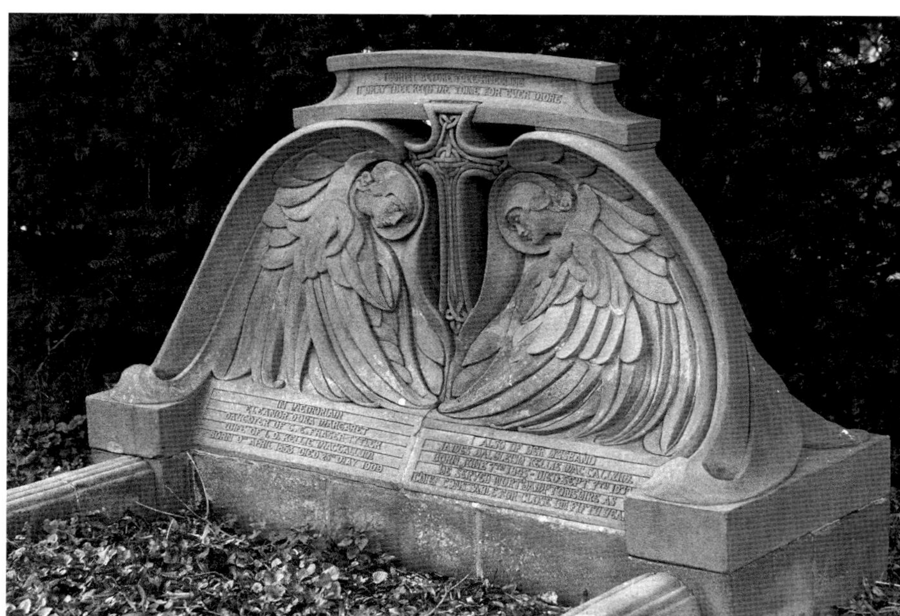

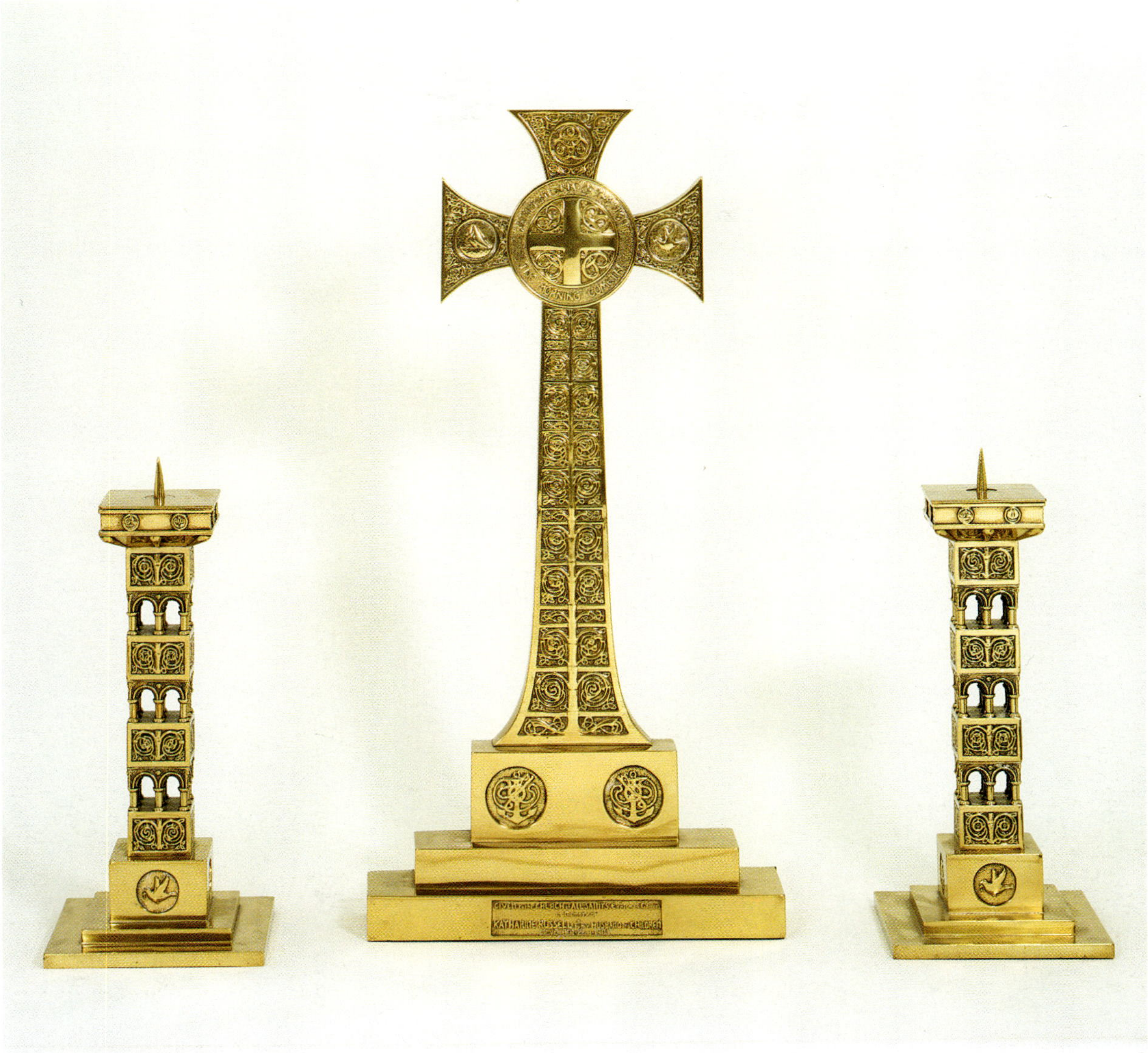

Cat 55. Altar Cross and Candlesticks, 1905, with Tree of Life imagery from the Watts Chapel, designed in memory of Katherine Russell, 1905

The Guild's first tombstone was inspired by a ninth-century wheel-shaped pattern in the Library of Saint Gall,[83] embellished by angels. Never more than than three feet high – except for the pilgrim's cross she erected in Signor's memory at Limnerslease and the Compton War Memorial (designed in consultation with Gertrude Jekyll) – their shape and symbolic decoration was in the form of knotwork or sensuous Art Nouveau angels whose flowing feathers on the backs of the memorials tightened into Art Deco style in the1920s and 1930s, as did the lettering which until then tended to be largely Celtic.

Among the earliest sundials was one inspired by a facetted dial at Holyrood Palace. Designed for Signor, it stood six foot high above an octagonal brick seat, and was inscribed with his motto; featuring sunflowers and the snake symbol of the sun, it was available from the Guild with alternative symbols and mottoes for the sum of £25. The four-foot Winged Hours sundial had angels facing north, south, east and west, smiling and frowning, for 'a touch of the human' as Mary observed;[84] and other sundials featured cobras, peacocks and owls. In 1901 she designed a memorial sundial to Queen Victoria richly ornamented with triangular dials reflecting light and shade – symbols of life and death – surmounted by an orb with the arms of England, Scotland, Wales and Ireland and four figures holding up a crown of Celtic hearts.

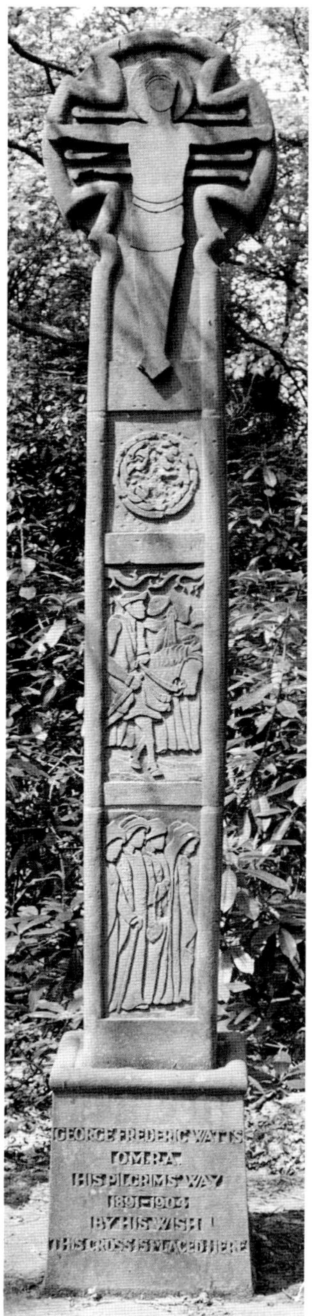

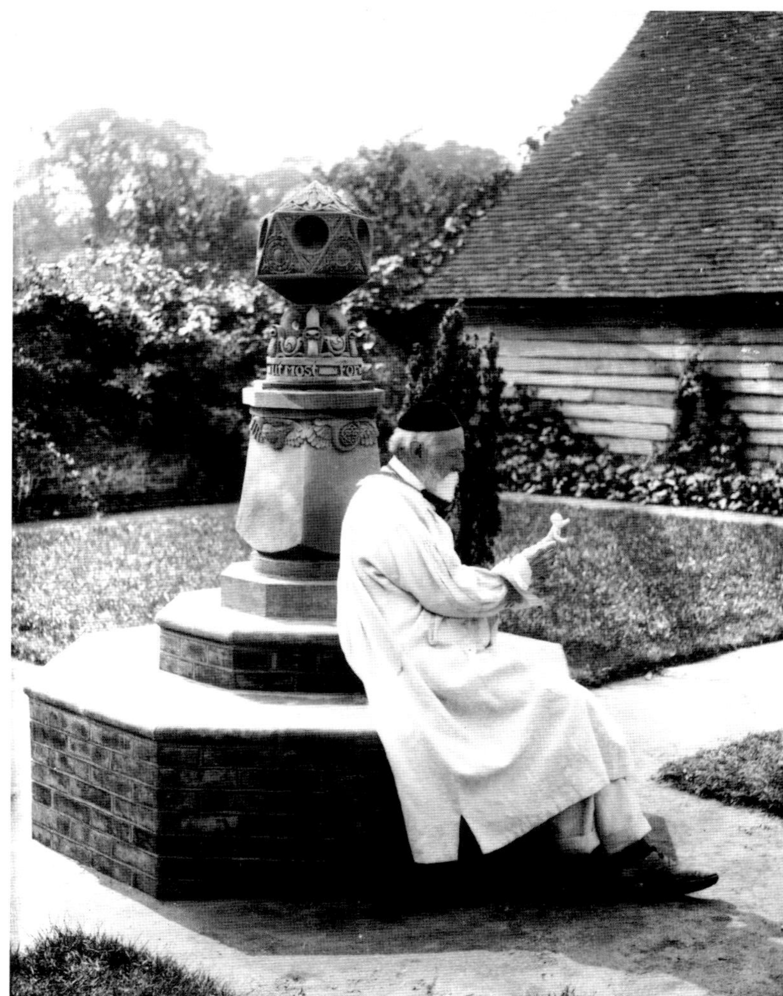

Below: 'His Pilgrims Way', Limnerslease
Right: Signor seated on 'The Utmost for the Highest' sundial, c1900

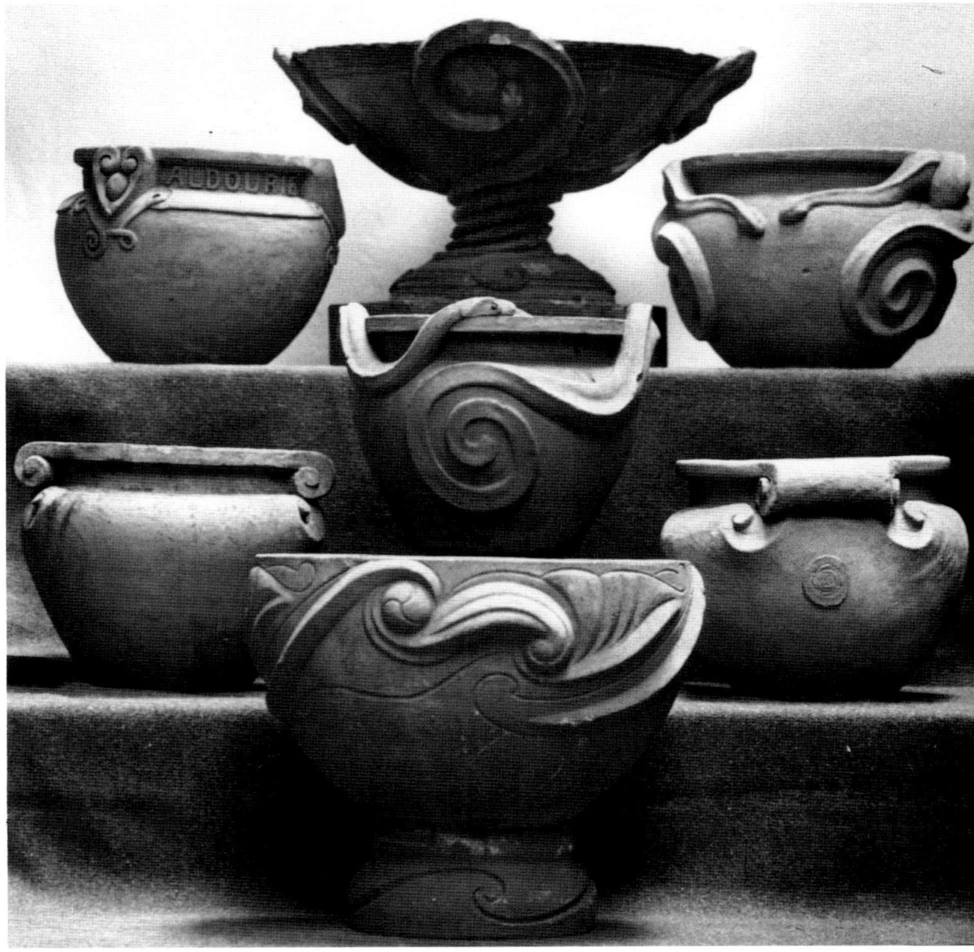

Right: Terracotta garden pots, Cats 83, 90, 86, 82, 81, 87
Below: Cat 74, Winged Hours Sundial, 1898

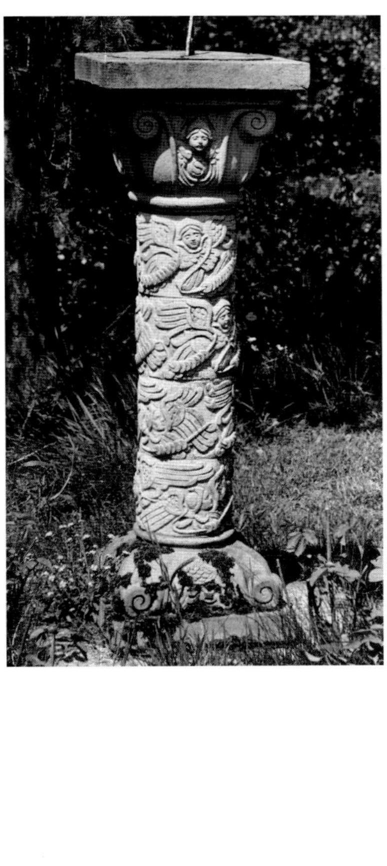

At the request of the Department of Agriculture and Technical Instruction for Ireland – 'to show what can be done with Irish raw material' – Mary's 'large garden vases decorated with Celtic designs' were shown in the 1904 Irish Industrial Exhibition at the World's Fair in St Louis, USA.[85]

Her architectural and garden ornaments produced by the Guild in red and grey terracotta were sold by Liberty's and awarded medals from the Royal Botanical and Royal Horticultural Societies. That Mary was acknowledged in Liberty catalogue while the name of their Celtic Revivalist designer Archibald Knox was omitted is testament not only to the standing of her husband, but to her forthright nature and views on the rights of women – yet she worked under the name of 'Mrs G F Watts'. In 1898 she sent a

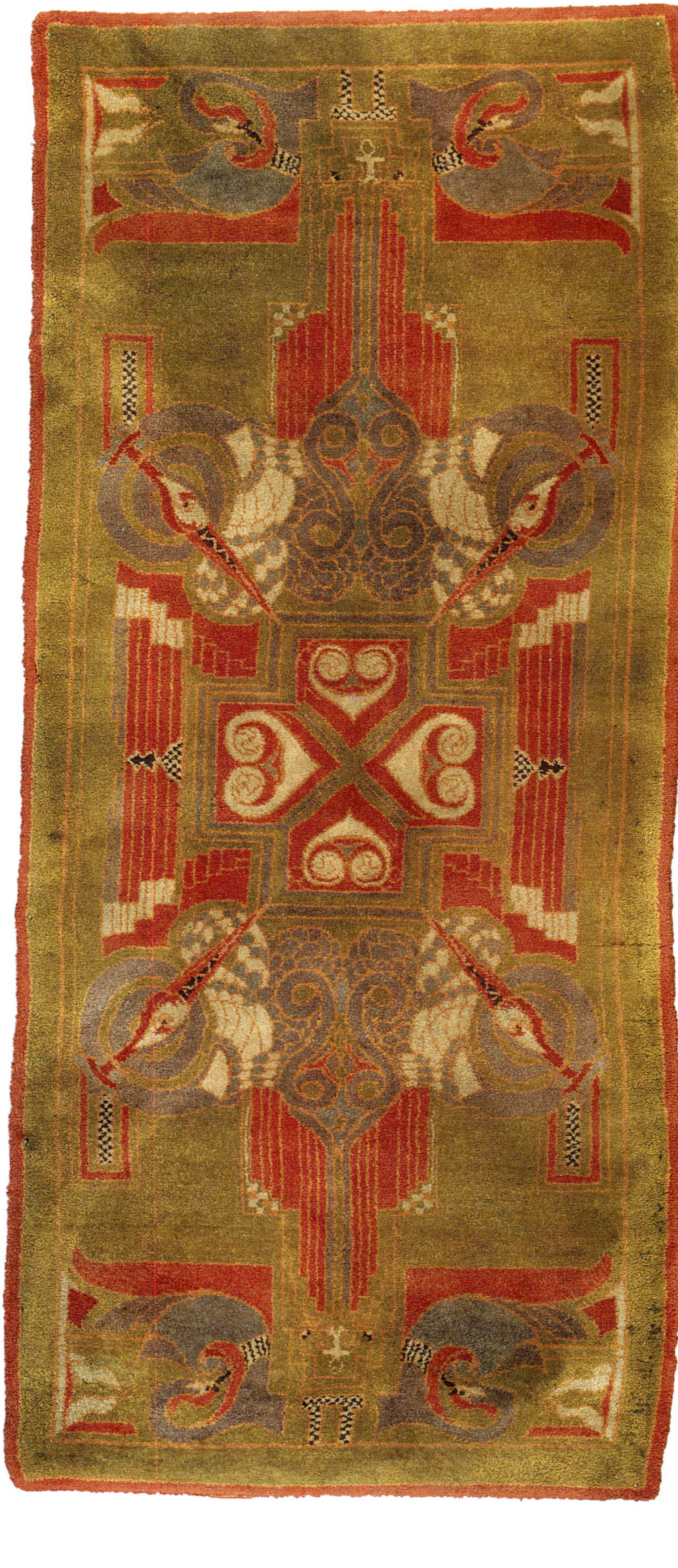

Cat 43. The Pelican Carpet, 1899-1901

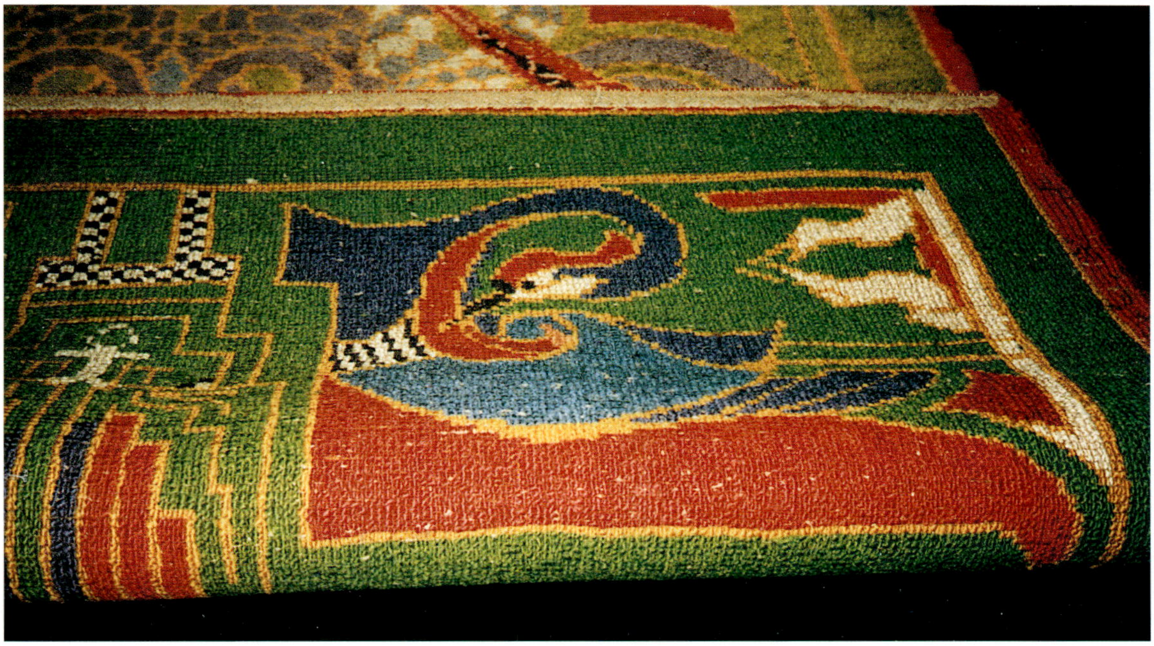

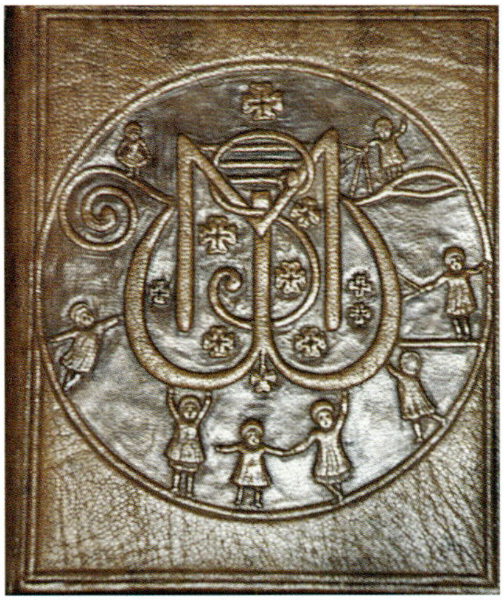

Above: Detail of Pelican on carpet reverse

Right: Cat 38. Bookbinding made to Mary's design by the Guild of Women Binders, 1897

design to be worked in *cuir bouilli* by the Guild of Women Binders, as a cover for Signor's exhibition catalogues. The following year she designed a symbolic rug to be woven at Killibegs in Donegal for Alexander Morton & Company and prompted James Morton to produce further Celtic-style carpets. The 2600 mm *Pelican* rug, a characteristically symbolic pattern of scrolling dragons, pelicans, hearts and poignant Key of Life, whose significance Mary explained in a detailed letter to the weavers (cat.45) was hand-tufted in wools of crimson, olive green and china blue and encompassed not only Mary's scrolling Celtic style and Art Nouveau forms, but anticipated an element of Art Deco. She lent Morton her facsimile copy of *The Book of Kells* and encouraged him to '*carry forward* the Celtic art' which she felt told only half the story and could be beautifully embroidered.

'There is no decoration so suited to *telling* its story. It is, I believe, like the gaelic language, the most emotional of the styles of decoration. But has the dangers common to all highly emotional things & requires temperance & judgement in the soul of the designer, to prevent it from becoming meaningless. I am sure with the revival of interest & pride in Celtic literature now so marked there will arrive, possibly from murky Glasgow, a young decoration master worthy to carry on in magnificent colour & in lively beautiful thought, the glory & the passionate flow of Celtic pattern.

'Far off & humbly it is on their lives I am trying to work – nothing in the chapel was *copied* except here & there, a single fine symbol, to be used for all time, like a gem, which reflects the light of any day that shines upon it – they drew out from their hearts as children do profound truths & did not half know how deep the well was from which they drew it.'[86]

The Pelican carpet featured in Liberty's Grafton Gallery exhibitions 'Founding a National Industry' (1903) of Donegal carpets and 'Modern Celtic Art' (1904), where the ride range of terracotta stamped with the Limnerslease wheelmark of the Compton Potters' Arts Guild was on show. (Liberty has revived Mary's design and the *Pelican Carpet Nepal* is available today at its Regent Street store.) In both catalogues Mary's pioneering role was acknowledged. 'Never before, in this country at least, has the Garden Pot been treated as an item, *per se*, of decorative skill,' wrote C J Ffoulkes. 'As in other branches of the applied arts, the present exhibitors have struck out into untrodden paths, and, in this instance largely aided and advised by Mrs G F Watts, the talented wife of our greatest living artist, having shown us what notable results can be achieved with simple forms treated with bold designs.'

Not only did the architectural enrichments combine well with practical horticultural shapes, but the weathered, porous terracotta drained well and withstood changes in temperature, and the Compton ware was frost-proof – the Aldourie clay weathered

Right: Cat 75. Capital of Owl Sundial, 1898

Below: Cat 106, Jekyll Bowl, 1908.

Bottom left: terracotta pots, cats 103, 108a, 102, 107a

Bottom right: detail of Winged Hours sundial

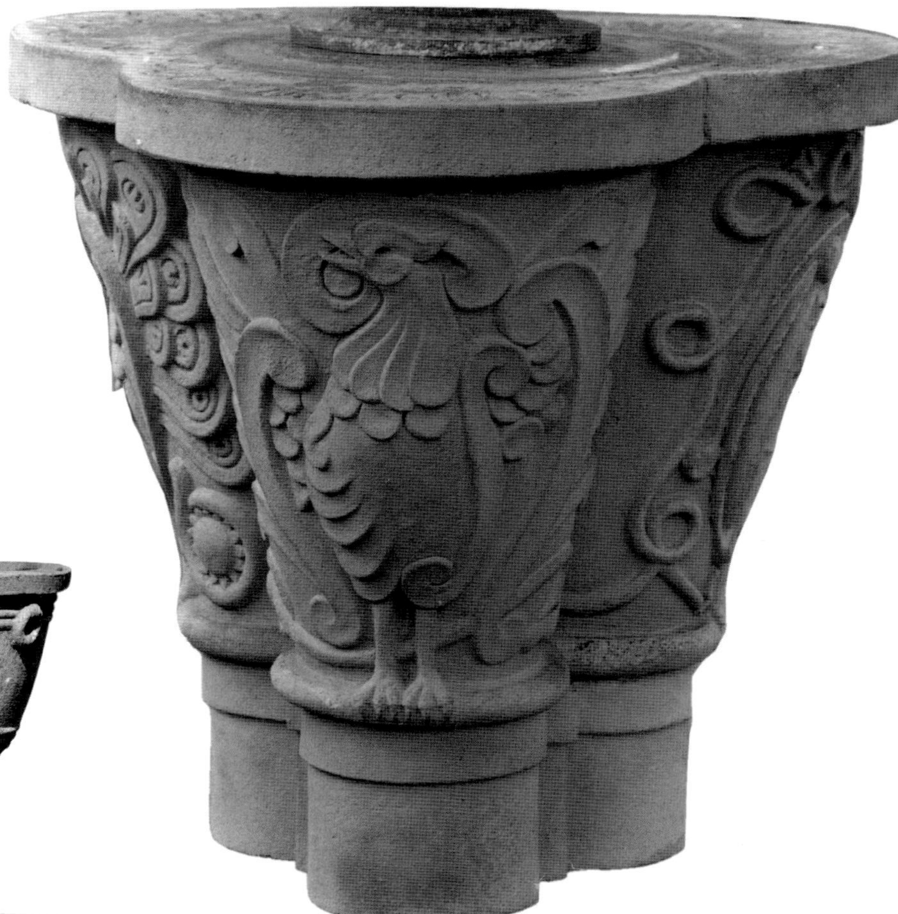

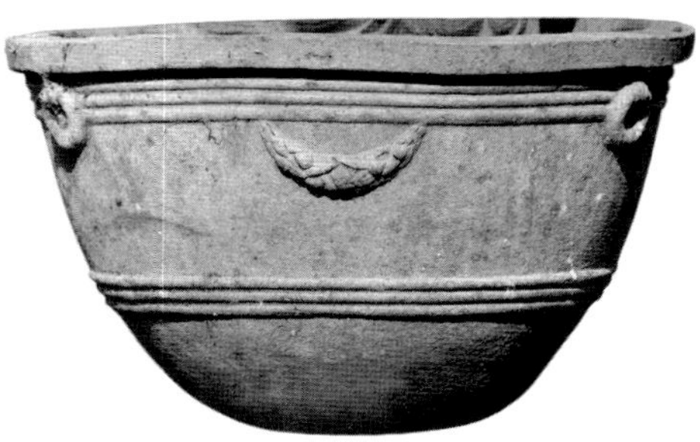

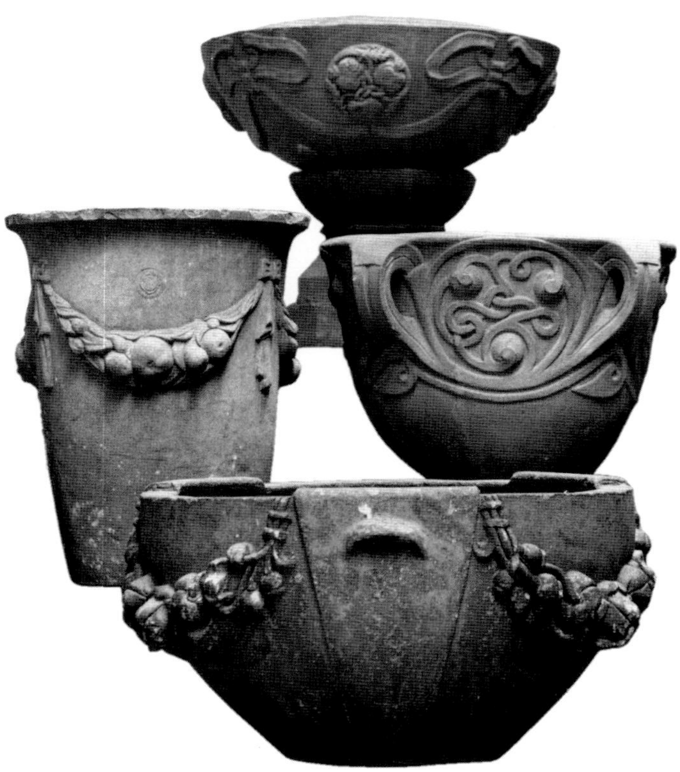

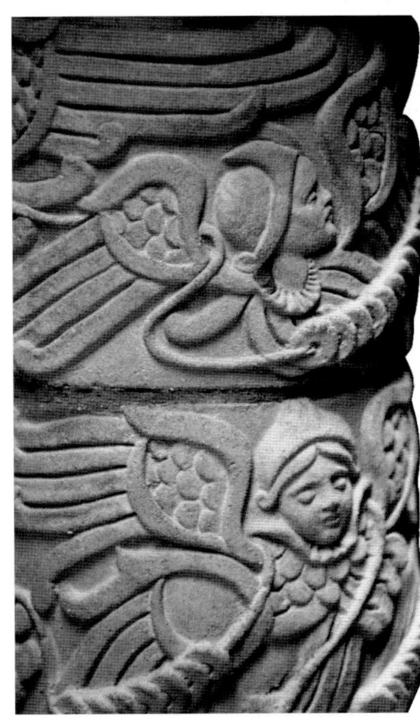

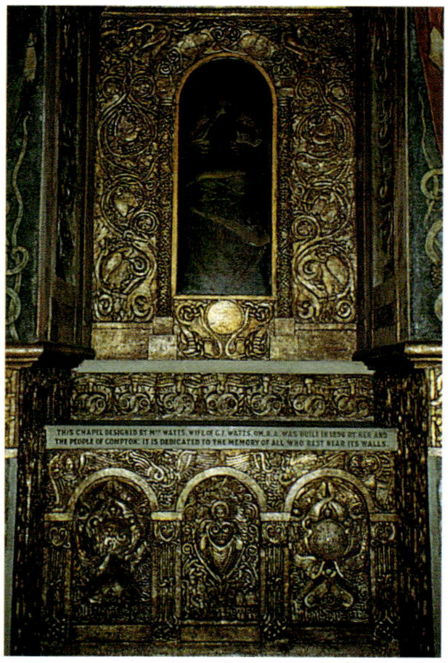

Watts Chapel Altar 1899

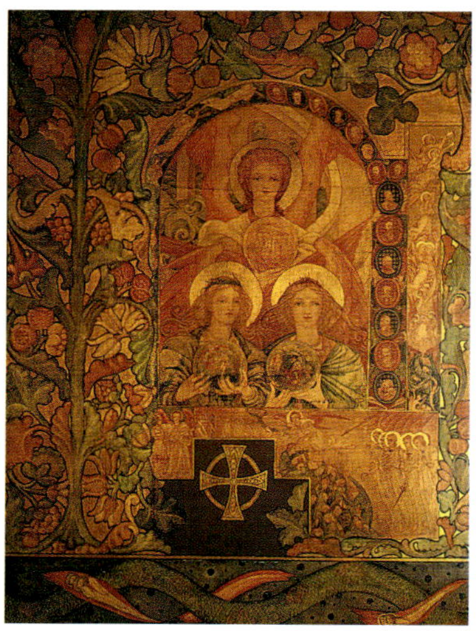

PHOEBE TRAQUAIR, Royal Hospital for Sick Children, Mortuary Chapel, Edinburgh, 1885-98

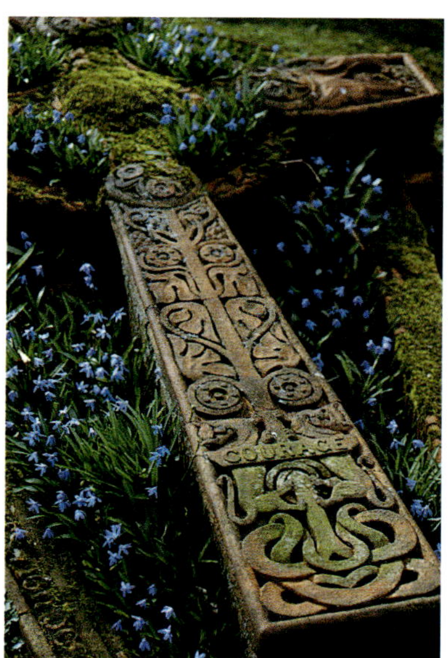

Memorial, 1901

less well. Wood fuel used in the kiln gave the material a delicate, broken hue. The deep cutting of Mary's relief decoration, encouraging mosaics of green moss, broadened her palette.

Of particular interest at the 'Modern Celtic Art' show were some 'Tiles for a Sanctuary Floor'. These were not used at Compton, or any other chapel with which we know she was involved.[87] Her design suggested 'the upward evolution of life. The outer circle shows a conventional treatment of plants and flowers, the next of fish, then beasts, birds, and in due sequence man, the stars, the angels, and in the centre encircling wings, the three symbols of the Highest. Each division of the design is parted by a plain surface suggesting a connecting pathway. And there is in addition a straight path to the centre, beset alternately with thorns and flowers.'[88]

By 1904 the interior decoration of the mortuary chapel at Compton was complete. Freer in style than the exterior and enriched with colour, organic Art Nouveau whiplash whirls in painted gesso relief over the circular walls, vaults and cross-ridge roof, becoming abstract on the window reveals. Only the lozenge-leaded glass, parquet floor and circular stone seats are undecorated. The roots of the Tree of Life – compact Celtic knots on the outer buttresses – have swelled into silvery tentacles floating around the oceanic blue-green drum. Glinting above, seraphim and cherubim clothed in reds, greens and golds draw the mourner's eye up through the girdle of the Trinity – gilded terracotta bas-relief patterns of Anglo-Saxon interlace with La-Tène- and Scandinavian-style bosses – through the branches of the vine towards the Eternal Circle of the sun. In the hands of the cherubim are jewel-like Art Nouveau medallions delicately bound by the Celtic cord. With a filigree effect achieved by applying piping cord to the stiff fibrous plaster, they resemble giant Ashbee pendants or Alexander Fisher enamels. Mary showed Fisher the decoration, and noted in her journal that he was more interested in line than symbolism, and found her cherubim too bright:

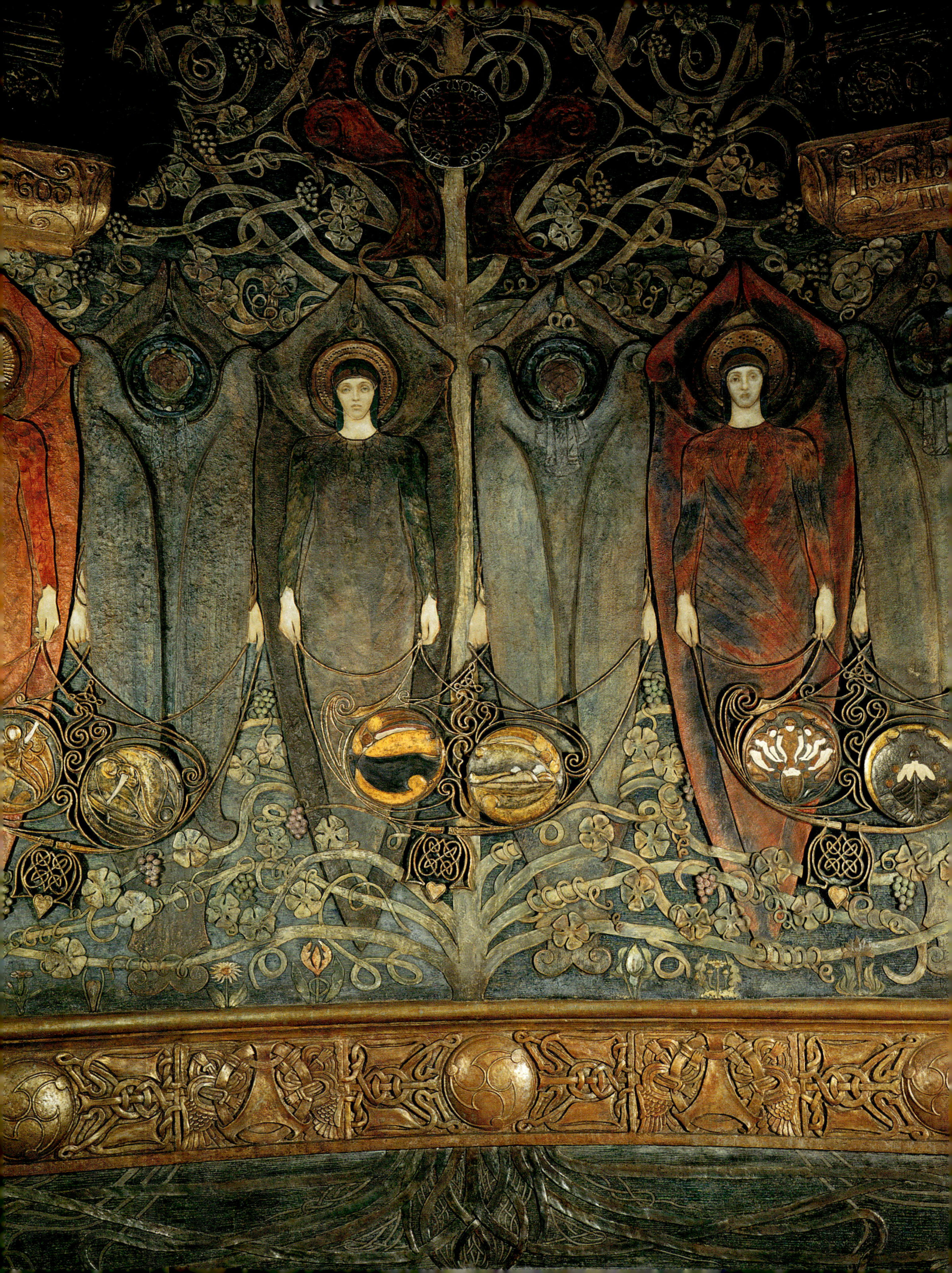

Mary working on the gesso panels

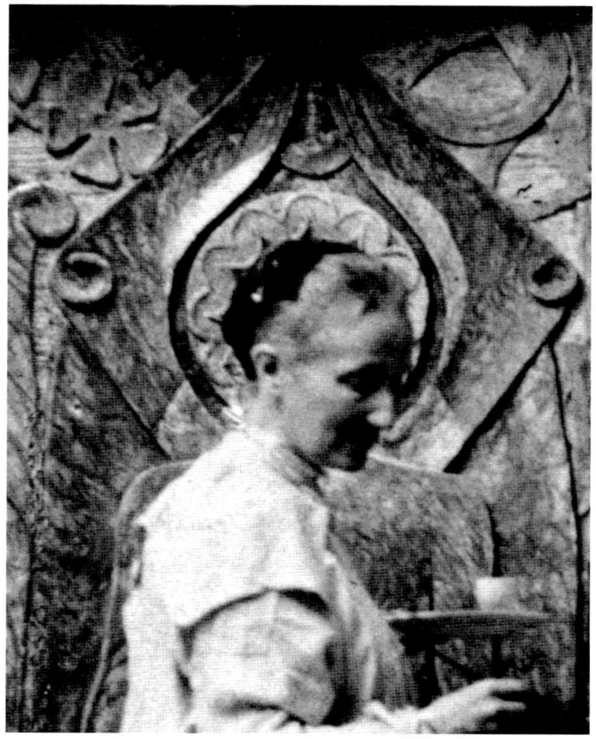

'His criticism is that the colour of the angels is not quite monotonous enough – I feel the same – it is astonishing that in the chapel light my green central angel has disappeared into the background, while the red and blue angel is bluer and redder than those in the studio – Of course the day was very dark.'[89]

Ribbons of winged cherub faces decorate the vaults and rise from golden corbels proclaiming, in Celtic-style lettering, the Immortality of the Soul.

The tightly modelled golden altar, with its arcuated frontal inspired by a *Kells* canon-table illumination, is surmounted by a dove frieze; and on the reredos is a small version of Signor's *The All-Pervading* (1904), his sole artistic contribution to the mortuary chapel. In its profuse organic ornamentation – or 'glorified wallpaper' as the Watts' described it – the interior bears a certain resemblance to a Rococo church, flowing in a continuous pattern from motif to motif, part gesso, part terracotta. But, like full-blown Art Nouveau, the Rococo style is asymmetric and, despite Mary's luxuriant calligraphic *fin-de-siècle* interior, her exuberant whiplash, almost reminiscent of Horta, remains symmetric.

Overleaf: Interior decoration in the Watts Chapel, 1901-4

It was closer in spirit to the work of the Arts and Crafts designer Phoebe Traquair, whose symbolic mural decoration of a mortuary chapel for the Royal Hospital for Sick Children in Edinburgh (1885-1898. See page 56) was inspired by medieval

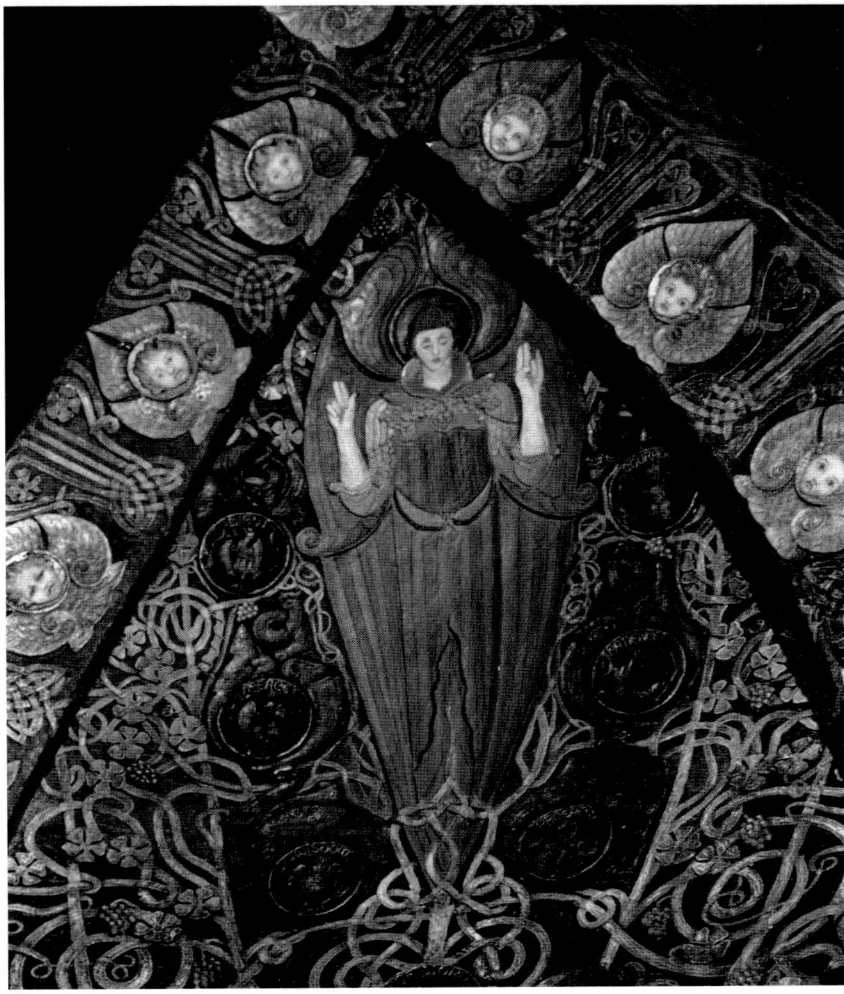

A seraph within ribbons of cherub faces inside the Watts Chapel

illuminations and the art of Dante Gabriele Rossetti. Traquair idolised Signor, and had visited Little Holland House. Mary, who had not at this stage seen her Edinburgh decorations (she may have seen them reproduced in *The Studio*), did not discuss her own work – except under the pretext of seeking advice for a friend, when she learned that Traquair painted in the Pre-Raphaelite tradition, over a thick ground of Chinese white.[90] Her transparent colour glows, though it does not vibrate like Mary's paint surface, and the texture is altogether smoother.

The colours used in the decoration of the Watts Chapel interior are those that appear on the terracotta household ware subsequently produced by the Compton Potters' Arts Guild, waxed and stamped with a small circular mark 'P.A.G.' (changed after her

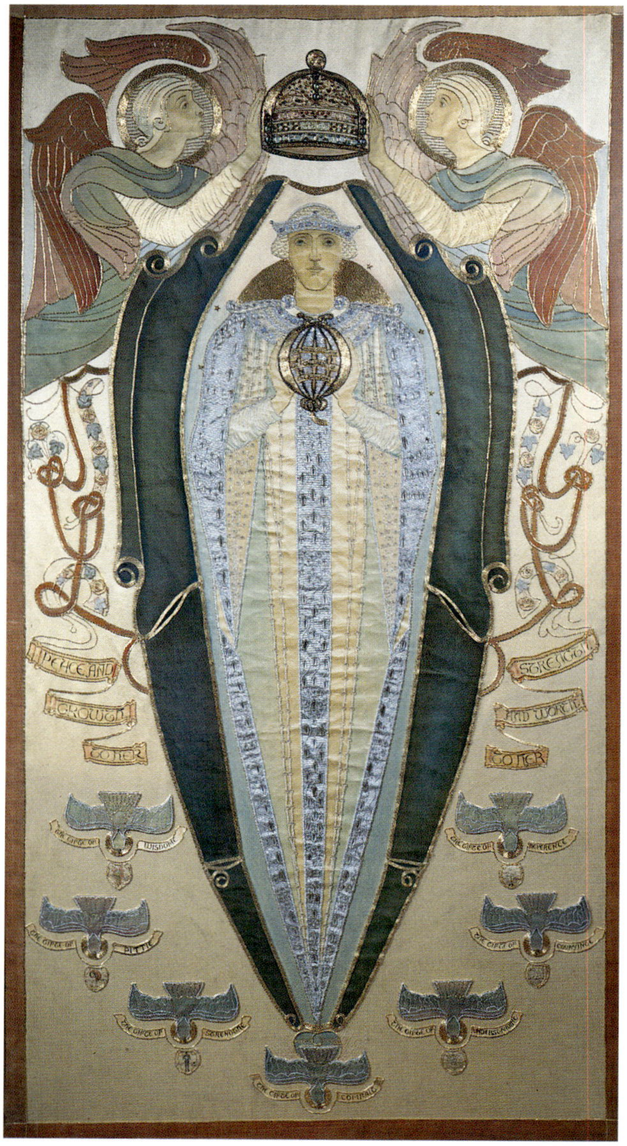

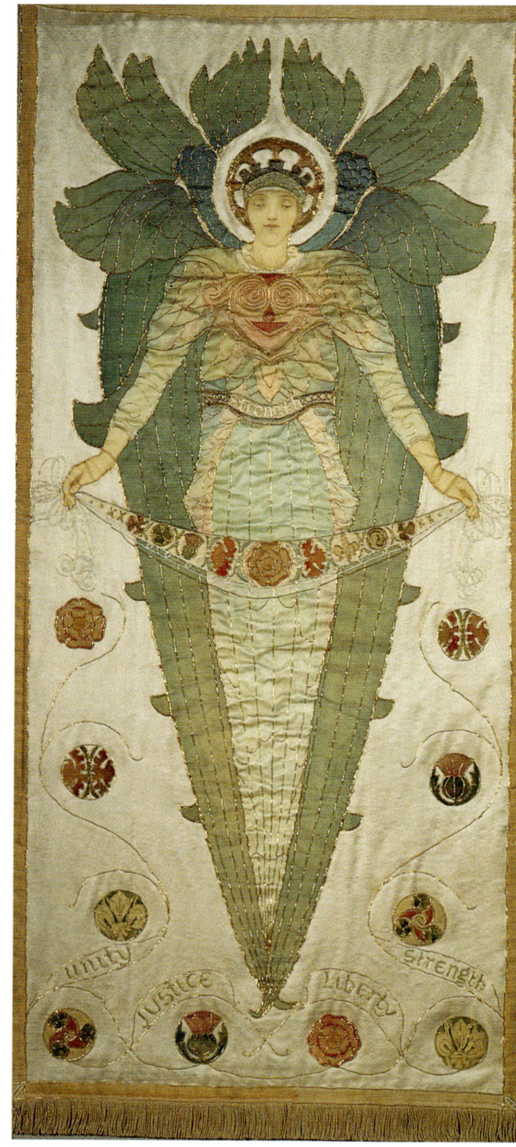

Above: Cat 64. Our Lady of the Snows, 1903
Right: Cat 67. Spirit of the Flowers of the Nations, 1907

Opposite: Cat 110. Cambridge Military Chapel, Aldershot. Detail of altarpiece, 1916-21

death to 'Compton Pottery'). For most of her later work, Mary drew on the iconographic vocabulary she had established in her decorative schemes at Limnerslease and the Watts Chapel. The seraph motif was worked into her designs for two marvellous embroidered banners commissioned by Earl Grey, the Governor General of Canada *Our Lady of the Snows* (1906) presented by Queen Alexandra to the Royal Victoria College, McGill University and *The Spirit of the Flowers of the Nations* which hung in Government House, Ottawa and is now in store at the Victoria &

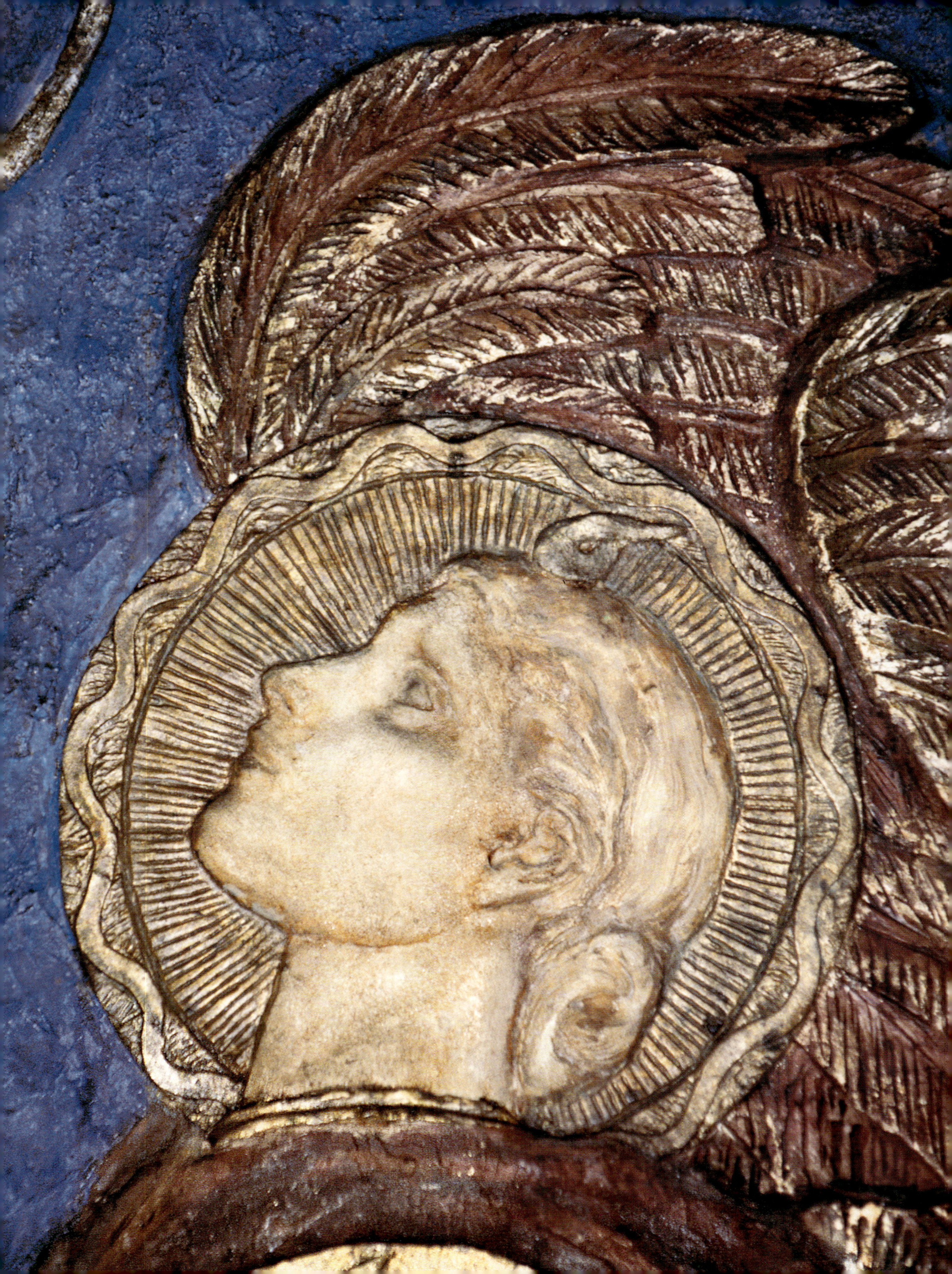

Albert Museum. Silk and velvet motifs painted in the graduated style of the Guild's coloured ware, were applied on to a satin ground, laid and couched with gold and silver thread outlines. The effect is quite unusual. As she began to design the Queen's banner, Mary wrote in her journal:

'I want to put everything into it, that can possibly be thought out. A full rounded aspiration to the give the children there . . . Our Lady of the Snows, is in the heart of it & to her heart she holds the central thought—the aspiration after the Divine, a chalice – this must be [diagram of flaming heart] the flame in the soul. She is to be crowned by Faith by Hope by Charity – a triple crown – She to sail on her mighty water, & her ship is led by seven doves, the seven giftes of the spirit – "The spirit of the years to come" may be the legend written below. I design piece meal! The crown & the dove.'[91]

Our Lady of the Snows accords largely with her original idea. However, in her hands the central motif is a pomegranate 'THE GOOD SEED ARE THE CHILDREN OF THE KINGDOM' and the flaming heart, which appears encrusted in jewels in the crown became the central motif of her second banner. Designed in 1907 – the year Mary was appointed Honorary President of the Women's Guild of Arts – the flowing wings of *The Spirit of the Flowers of the Nation* are characteristic of her later memorials. The Garment of Praise from the spandrels above the chapel door, which in itself resembles an embroidered wall-hanging and symbolizes Isaiah's comfort for the bereaved,[92] was used to decorate the Dores Memorial Arch (erected 1921, now partially destroyed), near Aldourie. Made by the Aldourie Potters' Arts Guild, the arch commemorates the fallen of the First World War, including some of its modellers, whose loss brought about the closure of the Guild in the Highlands.[93]

As Mary's brother Edward Fraser Tytler was a founder member of the Lovat Scouts, she roughed out a design for a silvered bronze casket to present to the officers on their return

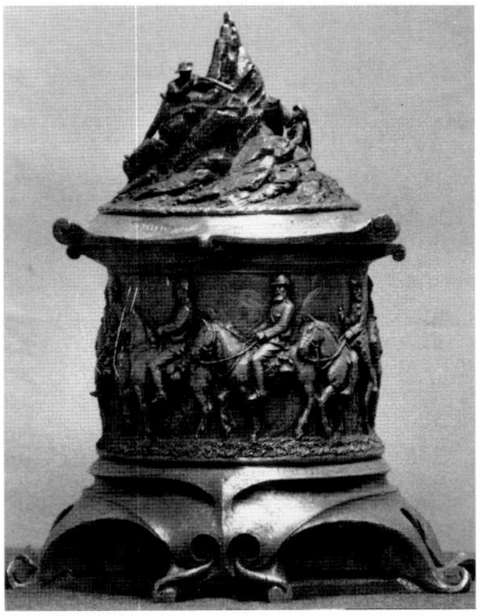

Above: Cat 68. LOUIS DEUCHARS, Lovat Scouts Casket, 1902

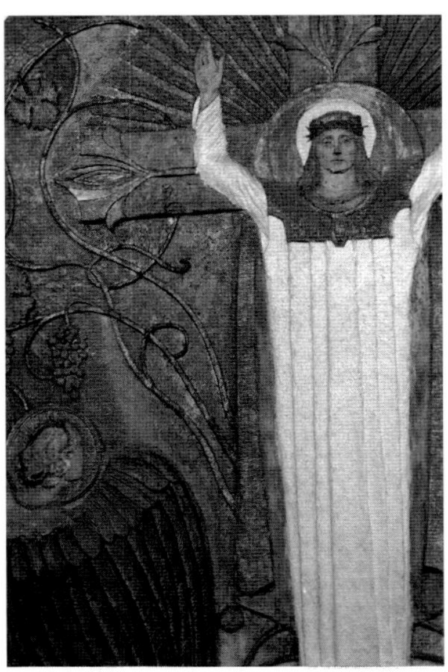

Below: Detail of Croix Fleuri on the Aldershot altarpiece

from the Boer War in 1902. Only the base seems to have been her work; and Louis Deuchars, whom she had poached from Signor's studio, trained to model terracotta to assist her classes for the chapel and sent up to run the Aldourie workshop, carried out the commission. Each officer was represented on horseback around the circular casket, and on its lid, the figure of Kenny Macdonald, the adjutant, lay on a South African *kopje*, peering through his telescope.

During the First World War she was asked by the Cambridge Military Hospital at Aldershot to design a symbolic frieze and altar decoration in painted gesso for their mortuary chapel. Her theme, the Progress of the three holy men from the Fiery Furnace of Suffering to the Song of Grace and the Glory of the Hereafter,[94] was to be carried out by the Compton Potters' Arts Guild under her supervision. The head and arms of Christ above the altar were modelled by her chief modeller Thomas Wren, but as the Guild members were called up for military service, she herself took over the project.

It was a heroic labour of love, for Mary was over seventy by the time the gesso work was finished. Yet she surely relished it. Her relief modelling is more sculptural, Pre-Raphaelite in style, featuring the odd Grecian or contemporary hairstyle. Little remains of the Celtic element – just the Tree of Life on the altar frontal and delicate entrelac above the altar, framing the arms of the symbolic *Croix Fleuri*, or 'Blossoming Cross'. The Celtic cord has become a ribbon of lettering weaving over the laps of the seated or kneeling winged figures. Her characteristic iconography is represented: the dove, peacock, vine, pomegranate – a heart casting out its seed for the renewal of life eternal – the alpha and omega, so clear and simple here within the circle surrounding the small central cross on the altar frontal, compared with the Celtic / Art Nouveau enrichments on the Compton doorway pillars. Above all, there is a greater sense of movement in the luscious wings, hands and folds of the drapery on the figures who play an

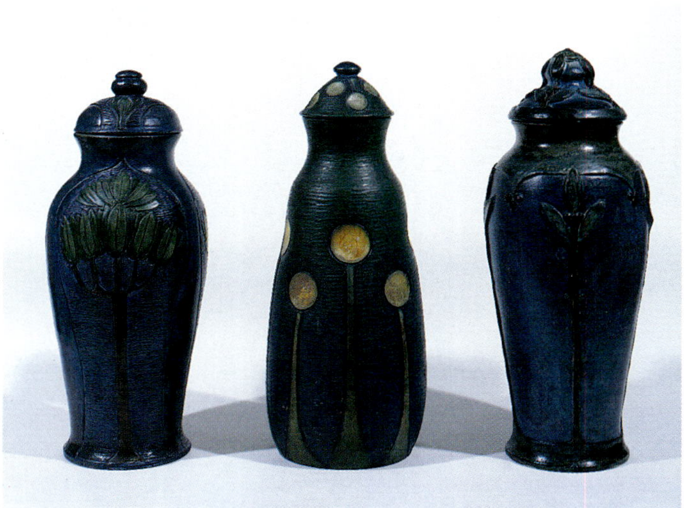

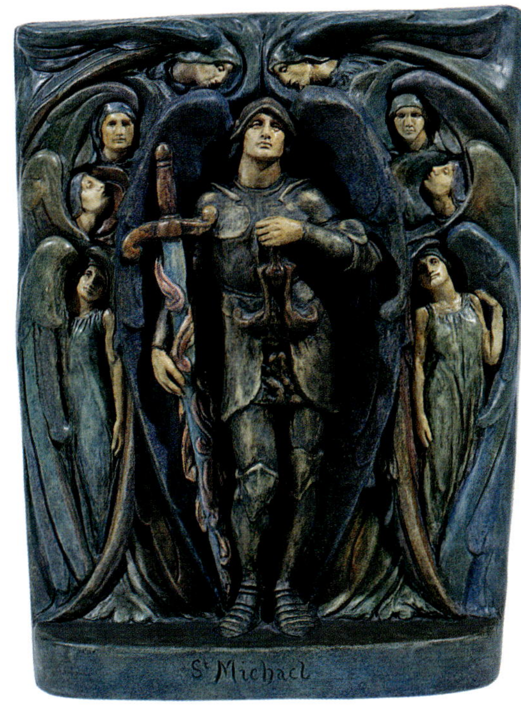

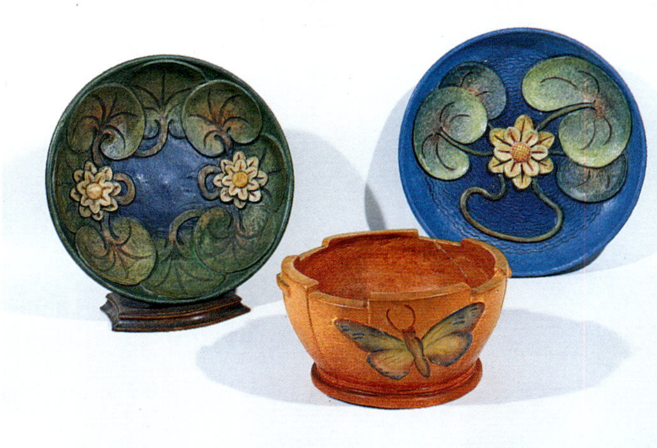

Compton Potters' Arts Guild

Coloured ware

Above left: Cats 130, 131, 129

Above right: Cat 116

Centre: Cats 144, 146, 145

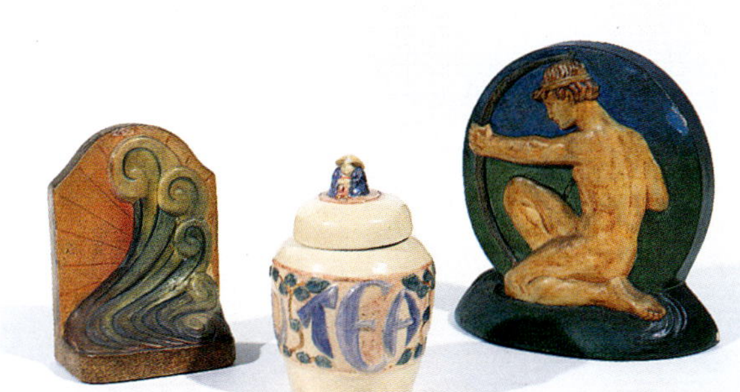

Above: Cats 143, 128, 142

Right: Cats 118, 123, 119

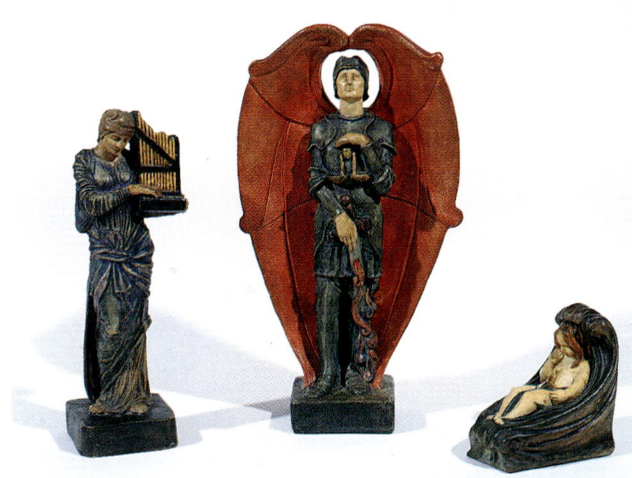

exuberant part in the narrative. (The Watts Gallery plans to re-erect these panels, saved when the Aldershot chapel was demolished.)

The underlying aim of Mary's work was to revive the best traditions in craftsmanship, to enhance the lives of ordinary people by opening their eyes to the beauty of art and educating them to become professional craftsmen and -women in their own right. Her crusading championship of the Home Arts, with Signor, contributed to the development of today's adult education classes. As A H Mackmurdo wrote:

'Had it not been for the work done by the Home Arts and Industries Association, it may be questioned whether the Art Workers' Guild, or the Council craft schools would have yet been established. Personal and private initiative is always the forerunner of corporate and public institution. These schools, then, we should regard as the first fruits of the Arts and Crafts Movement.'[95]

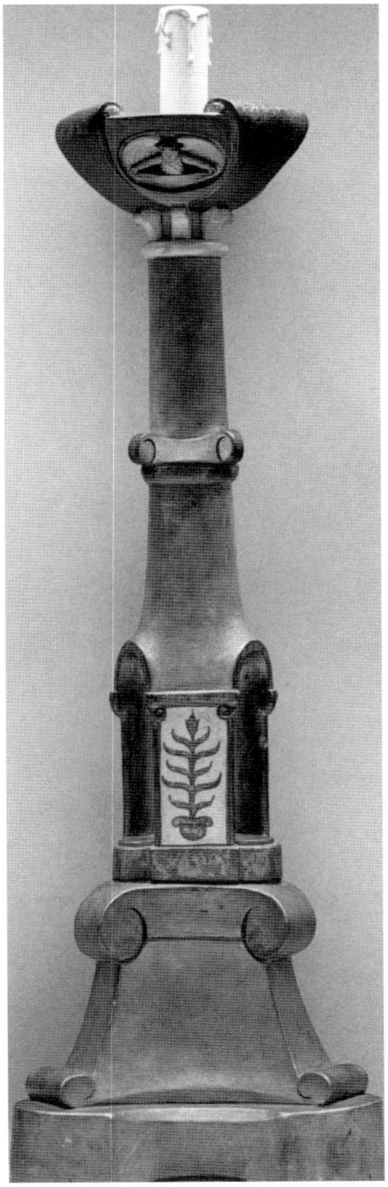

Cat 127. Candlestick lamp, 1910

Through her extraordinary imagination and courage in the face of doubters, and of course privileged access to experts, Mary Watts enabled the villagers of Compton to create their own legacy, the Watts Chapel. Although the concept and design were her own, without Signor's support, the chapel could not have been built. As artists and symbolists, they were partners. He trained her, and whereas his paintings were undecorated in order to appeal to all nations, she extended the principle with decorative imagery relating to worldwide civilizations.

After Signor's death in 1904, Mary's team of potters, throwers, modellers, colourists and mould-makers under the management of James Nicol – carried out architectural work for Edwin Lutyens and Clough Williams Ellis, in addition to the memorials, household and terracotta ornaments decorating gardens throughout Britain and abroad. Tiny versions of their jardinières were commissioned by Gertrude Jekyll for Queen

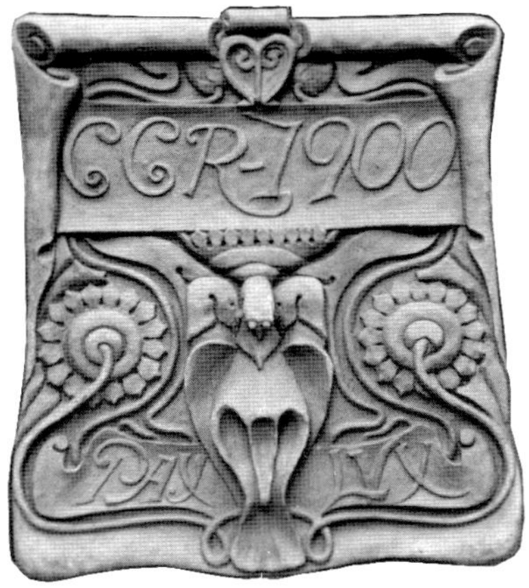

Above: Cottage plaque, 1900

Below left: Detail of Wellhead, 1906

Right: Watts Memorial Cloister, 1912

Mary's Dolls House in 1921. Production continued under the management of one of her first apprentices George Aubertin – long after Mary died, aged 88, on 6 September 1938. When Compton Pottery was taken over by the broadcaster David Dunhill, Aubertin appeared in the television *Interlude* shaping a pot on the wheel. The pottery finally closed in 1955.

Every aspect of her potters' work during her lifetime had symbolic meaning, from the shape of a pot, to a wall plaque, finial, commemorative pendant, or a motto. Mary's father had sown the seeds in her fertile mind, nurtured during her marriage to Signor, when sinuous spirals of clay and gesso flowered into schemes of mysterious significance.

Her response to a criticism of symbolism in her husband's work surely applies to her own:

'As long as symbolism does not force itself disagreeably upon you, by the sacrifice of the finest principles that art should be beautiful, delightful, reticent, no man can make it too interesting.'[96]

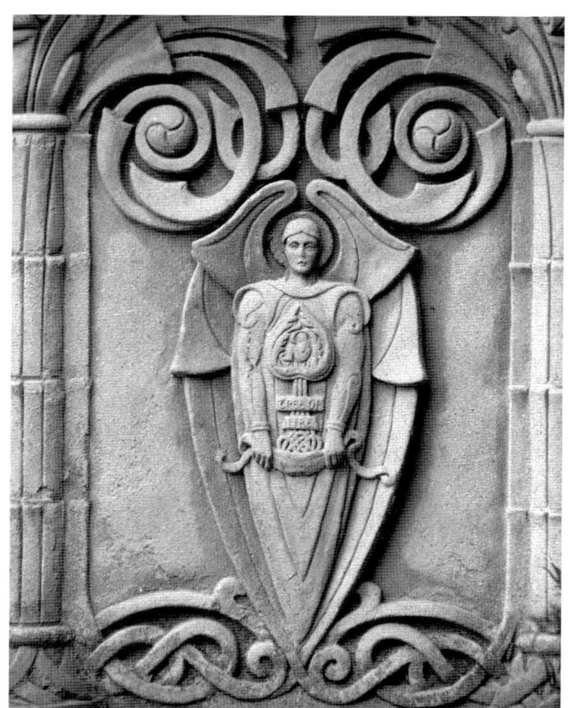

Notes

[1] Letter from Mary Seton Watts, Limnerslease, to James Morton, 15 March 1901, National Art Archives ref: AAD 4/520 1978)
[2] A style of Celtic art 5th-1st century BC, founded in Switzerland and spread through central Europe to Britain
[3] MARY SETON WATTS, *George Frederic Watts: The Annals of an Artist's Life*, Macmillan & Co Ltd, London, 1912, (3 vols) I, 287-88
[4] ibid, 122
[5] Letter from Anne Thackeray Ritchie to Walter Senior, ed HESTER RITCHIE, *Letters of Anne Thackeray Ritchie*, 1924, 125-26
[6] ALFRED, LORD TENNYSON 'The Princess: A Medley', published 1847
[7] MSW, *op cit*, I, 205-6
[8] WILLIAM ALLINGHAM The Diaries, ed H Allingham & D Radford, The Folio Society, London, 164-5; MFT *Journal*, 20 June 1868
[9] MSW, *G F Watts, op cit*, I, 289
[10] *ibid*, I, 288-89
[11] *ibid*, I, 289-90
[12] ELIZABETH LONGFORD *Darling Loosy: Letters to Princess Louise 1856-1939,* Weidenfeld & Nicholson, London, 1991, 15
[13] E POYNTER *Lectures on Art* 'Systems of Art Education', 2 October 1871, Lecture III, 1879, quoted in ANDREW FORGE *The Slade 1871-1960*, 33-34
[14] MAURICE DREFOUS, *Dalou, sa vie et son oeuvre*, Paris, 1903, 69-70; SUSAN BEATTIE, *The New Sculpture,* Yale University Press, New Haven & London, 1983, 14-16; CHRISTOPHER FRAYLING, *The Royal College of Art: 150 Years of Art & Design*, Barrie & Jenkins, London, 1987, 55
[15] MSW, *Commonplace Book*, 17 September 1875
[16] MSW, *Journal*, 9 April 1876 (WG)
[17] *ibid*
[18] PINNINGTON, *op cit*, 2; George Paul Chalmers RSA & the Art of his Time (1838-78), *Art Journal*, 1897, 83-88
[19] Letter from MFT to GFW, Sanquhar, 14 March 1882, reprinted in CHAPMAN *The Laurel & the Thorn*, Faber & Faber Ltd, London, 1945, 112
[20] As F P Cockerell had died in 1878, GFW commissioned George Aitchison to design a gallery and make further alterations to LHH, completed by May 1881
[21] MSW Commonplace Book, December 1883 (WG)
[22] Letter from MFT, 68 Eccleston Square, SW2, to GFW, 26 January 1885, quoted in CHAPMAN, *op cit*, 113-14
[23] Mary Mead, later wife of Edwin Abbey
[24] Letter from GFW, 24 Lewes Crescent, Kemp Town, Brighton, to MFT, 27 January 1885, quoted in CHAPMAN, *op cit*, 114
[25] HENRIETTA BARNETT, *Canon Barnett: His Life, Work & Friends*, John Murray, London, 1918
[26] EGLYNTYNE JEBB, *Journal*; JEBB 'The Rights of Women', reprinted from *The Temperance Visitor*, 25 August 1882
[27] Lord Brownlow (president), Charles Leland, John Ryland, G R Redgrave, W A S Benson, Alfred Harris, Mrs McCallum, Miss Noyes, The Hon E Plunkett, Miss Hope, Mrs Robinson, Mrs Arthur Jebb, Walter Besant (treasurer), Miss Dymes (secretary); EJ's MS journal
[28] Journal of Eglantyne Jebb
[29] Letter from GFW to MFT, 31 March 1886, quoted in MSW, *G F Watts*, II, 58
[30] MFT *Commonplace Book* (WG)
[31] Presented in November 1896 to the National Portrait Gallery
[32] Presented in July 1897 to Henry Tate's new National Gallery of British Art
[33] Letter from GFW to MFT, 23 July 1886
[34] MFT *Commonplace Book* (WG)
[35] MSW, *G F Watts*, II, 63
[36] *ibid*, 3 October 1886
[37] MSW G F Watts II 71
[38] *Journal*, 24 January 1887
[39] *ibid*, 1 January 1887
[40] *ibid*, 17 February 1887 & MSW exercise book at WG
[41] *ibid*, 5 April 1887
[42] *ibid*, 22 April 1887
[43] *ibid* 5 June 1887
[44] *ibid*, 29-30 July, 4 October 1887

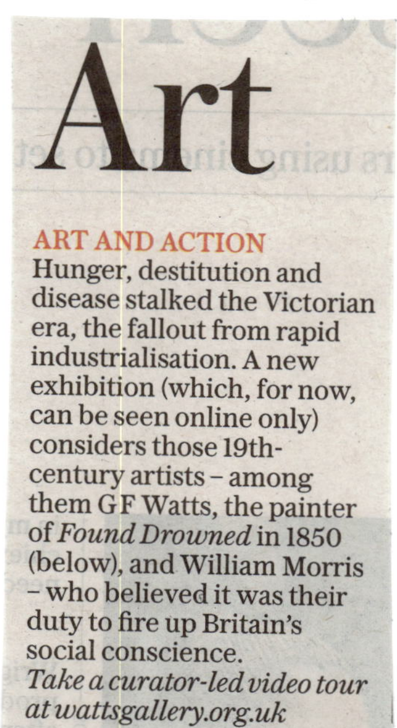
Art

ART AND ACTION
Hunger, destitution and disease stalked the Victorian era, the fallout from rapid industrialisation. A new exhibition (which, for now, can be seen online only) considers those 19th-century artists – among them GF Watts, the painter of *Found Drowned* in 1850 (below), and William Morris – who believed it was their duty to fire up Britain's social conscience.
Take a curator-led video tour at wattsgallery.org.uk

[45] *ibid*, 20 August 1887; *G F Watts* II, 85; letter from Edward Burne-Jones, The Grange, West Kensington, u/d 1887, to GFW (Watts Gallery microfiche 16, G8-9)
[46] *Journal Notes*, 27 August 1895
[47] *Journal*, 8 July 1887
[48] *ibid*, 11 August 1887
[49] *ibid*, 16 September 1887
[50] *ibid*, 7 September 1887
[51] MSW *G F Watts* II 137-38
[52] Letter from Sir Frederic Leighton, 2 Holland Park Road, 24 May 1889 (*The Leighton Letters*, No 12744 Kensington Local History Library)
[53] Letter from Sir Frederic Leighton to MSW (*The Leighton Letters*, No 12742); 'An Appeal Against Female Suffrage' *The Nineteenth Century*, No CXLVIII June 1889, 781-88; *G F Watts* II 145-46 and *Journal Notes* 23 May 1889
[54] MSW, *GF Watts*, II, 190
[55] WALTER CRANE 'Of Decorative Painting and Design', *Arts and Crafts Exhibition Society Catalogue of the First Exhibition*, The New Gallery, 1888, 32-33
[56] PATRICK GEDDES, *Every Man His Own Critic*, 1888, 50-51
[57] MSW *Journal* 25 Jan 1891
[58] *ibid*, 21 October 1896
[59] *ibid*, 12 March 1891
[60] *ibid*, 24, 30 August, 5 September, 5-6 October 1891
[61] *G F Watts* II 200
[62] *Journal*, 6 August 1891
[63] *ibid*, 31 January 1893
[64] *ibid*, 1 February 1893
[65] *ibid*, 18 May 1893
[66] CHAPMAN, op cit, 134
[67] MSW, *Journal*, 21 September 1891
[68] *ibid*, 28 February 1893
[69] *ibid*, 6, 7 August and 20 September 1891; MSW's notes on Prometheus read, 'Climb, Attains. Is chained, and is Redeemed.'
[70] *The Westminster Budget*, 27 November 1894
[71] ANNY THACKERAY RITCHIE *Journal*, March 1896
[72] MSW, *Journal*, 2, 9, 10, 15 January & 13 March 1893
[73] *ibid*, 3 & 13 August 1893
[74] *ibid* 22 October 1891
[75] *ibid*, 1 October 1893
[76] 'First Law in Decoration' in MSW MS notebook
[77] VERONICA FRANKLIN, *The Watts Chapel: An Arts & Crafts Memorial*, 1993
[78] MSW, *The Word in the Pattern*, William H Ward, London, 1899, 5
[79] Proverbs, IV, 18
[80] *The Book of Durrow* (Trinity College Dublin MS A 4.5./MS57) f3v
[81] MSW, *The Word in the Pattern*, *op cit*, 25-26; VFG, *op cit*, 16-17
[82] *The Studio*, VIII, 1896
[83] Commencement of Penitential from the Library of St Gall, Code No 1395, reproduced in J O WESTWOOD, *Facsimiles of the Miniatures & Ornaments of Anglo-Saxon & Irish Manuscripts*, Bernard Quaritch, London, 1848, plate 28
[84] MSW, *Journal*, 30 March 1898
[85] *Irish Industrial Exhibition, World's Fair St Louis 1904*, Handbook and Catalogue to Industrial Section, 31 & 35
[86] Letter from MSW, Limnerslease, 15 March 1901, to James Morton (National Archive of Art & Design)
[87] The St Alban's Workhouse chapel (now destroyed), Stoke Rochford Church, Cambridge Military Chapel, Aldershot
[88] *Modern Celtic Art*, Liberty's Grafton Gallery catalogue, 1903
[89] MSW *Journal*, 7 December 1902
[90] Letter from Phoebe Traquair, 5 Dean Park Crescent, to MSW, u/d [probably 1898]
[91] MSW, *Journal*, 29 July 1906
[92] Isaiah, LXI, 1-3
[93] 'Dores Memorial Arch'. *Inverness Courier*, 20 September 1921
[94] Daniel, III
[95] A H MACKMURDO, *History of the Arts and Crafts Movement* (MS in William Morris Gallery, Walthamstow)
[96] *ibid*, 12 April 1891

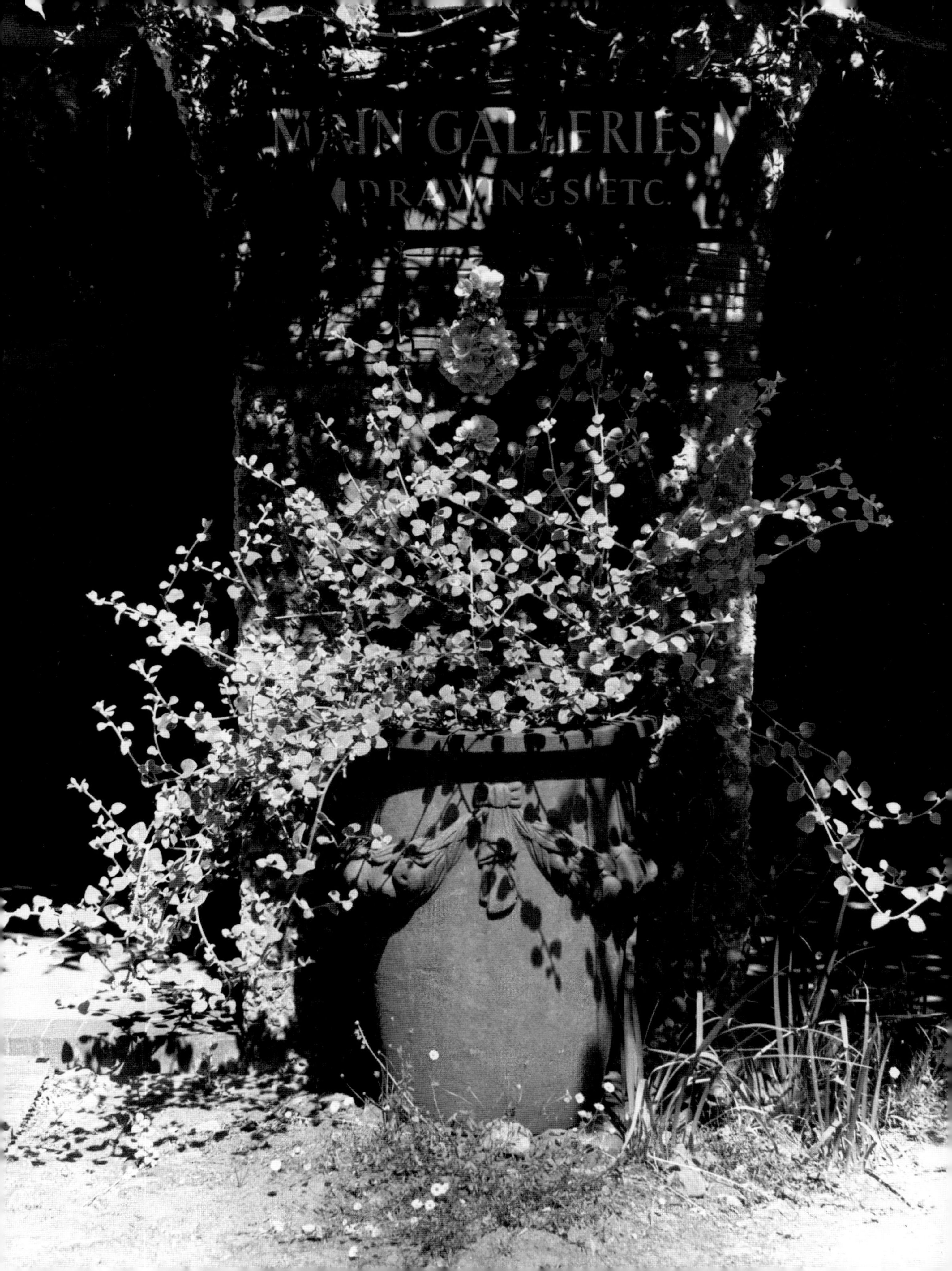
MAIN GALLERIES
DRAWINGS ETC.

The Catalogue

Julia Margaret Cameron, Dalou, Portraits, George Paul Chalmers

Brought up at Aldourie Castle in Inverness-shire, Mary Fraser-Tytler was a skilled watercolourist by the age of eighteen. In 1868, she sat for and assisted the photographer Julia Margaret Cameron at Freshwater. She studied art in Dresden and Rome, and on her return to England in 1870, visited Watts's studio for the first time. After attending the National Art-Training School at South Kensington and The Slade, she studied claymodelling with Aimée-Jules Dalou and portrait painting with Watts. In 1876, she sat to the Scottish Academician George Paul Chalmers.

CAT 1
JULIA MARGARET CAMERON
(1815-79)
Rosebud Garden of Girls
Albumen, 1868
30 x 27.3 cm
Private Collection

CAT 2
MARY SETON FRASER TYTLER
(1849-1938) and JULIA MARGARET
CAMERON (1815-79)
Prince Alamayu of Abyssinia
Albumen and watercolour, 1868, signed on opposite leaf by Prince Alamayu and Captain Speedy
34.3 x 27 x 3 cm
Private Collection

CAT 3
JULIA MARGARET CAMERON
(1815-79)
Whisper of the Muse
print from old glass negative, 1865
11.4 x 10 cm
Watts Gallery

CAT 4
MARY SETON FRASER TYTLER
(1849-1938)
Mother and Child
Terracotta, 1873-79
31.5 cm high
Watts Gallery

CAT 5
MARY SETON FRASER TYTLER
(1849-1938)
Mrs Edward Liddell
Oil on canvas, 1870
Inscribed on stretcher 'Christiana Catherine Fraser-Tytler, daughter of Charles Edward Fraser-Tytler Esq. Mrs Edward Liddell (1870). M Fraser Tytler (p)
61.6 x 51.1 cm
Private Collection

CAT 6
MARY SETON FRASER TYTLER
(1849-1938)
Etheldred Fraser Tytler
oil on canvas, 1875
63 x 53 cm
Private Collection

CAT 7
MARY SETON FRASER TYTLER
(1849-1938)
Mrs Edward Liddell
watercolour, 1877, signed C.C. Liddell by MFT June 18 77
33 x 33 cm
Private Collection

CAT 8
GEORGE PAUL CHALMERS RSA
(1833-78)
Mary Fraser Tytler
Oil on canvas, 1876
45.8 x 35.6 cm
Private Collection

CAT 9
MARY SETON FRASER TYTLER
(1849-1938)
Self-Portrait
Oil on canvas, signed with MFT monogram and dated 1881
68 x 55.2 cm
Private Collection

CAT 10
MARY SETON FRASER TYTLER
(1849-1938)
Self-Portrait
Watercolour, 1882
50.3 x 35 cm
Watts Gallery

CAT 11
MARY SETON FRASER TYTLER
(1849-1938)
Miss Eden
Oil on canvas, signed MFT 1882
61 x 51 cm
Private Collection160

CAT 12
Mary Fraser Tytler's studio at Sanquhar
photograph
11.2 x 17.8 cm
Private Collection

CAT 13
Aldourie
watercolour, 1886
34 x 49 cm (59 x 74 cm framed)
Private Collection

CAT 14
MARY SETON FRASER TYTLER
(1849-1938)
Commonplace Book
18.9 x 12 cm
Watts Gallery

Marries Watts, Little Holland House

On marriage to Watts in 1886, Mary abandoned easel-painting and turned to decorative art, designing bas-reliefs to symbolize Wattsian thought.

CAT 15
GEORGE FREDERIC WATTS (1817-1904)
Mary Seton Watts
Oil on canvas, 1887
88.9 x 76.2 cm
Private Collection

CAT 16
GEORGE FREDERIC WATTS (1817-1904)
Mary Seton Watts
Oil on canvas, 1887
41.5 x 36.2 cm
Watts Gallery

CAT 17
MARY SETON WATTS (1849-1938)
Journal
7–8 June 1887
13 x 11 cm
Watts Gallery

CAT 18
Mr and Mrs George Frederic Watts in the studio at Little Holland House, Kensington
Photograph, 1887
29.5 x 21 cm
Watts Gallery

CAT 19
MARY SETON WATTS (1849-1938)
Watts's Seal and Bookplate, 'The Utmost for the Highest'
1888
9.2 x 4.8 x 2.2 cm
Watts Gallery

CAT 20
The left hands of George Frederic and Mary Seton Watts
Plaster, 1889
12.5 x 29 x 12 cm
Watts Gallery

Limnerslease

For her symbolic decorative schemes at Limnerslease, the house built for the Watts at Compton by Ernest George in 1891, Mary began to research the art of ancient civilizations. Gesso ceilings, Watts' exotic reading alcove, brass and terracotta fire surrounds show the development of her vibrant Celtic style – her principal source was *The Book of Kells* – which she infused with Art Nouveau forms of her day. Both the Watts intended their art to have universal appeal, but whereas Watts sought to paint a clear message undiluted by decoration, Mary sought to include worldwide pantheistic imagery in her bas-reliefs.

CAT 21a & 22b
MARY SETON WATTS (1849-1938)
Plans for The Red Room Ceiling at Limnerslease
1891
Watts Gallery

CAT 22
MARY SETON WATTS (1849-1938)
The Red Room Ceiling at Limnerslease
Gesso, 1891
Watts Gallery

CAT 23
Plans for Watts Ceiling at Limnerslease
1891
Watts Gallery

CAT 24
MARY SETON WATTS (1849-1938)
'The Utmost for the Highest' Watts's Ceiling at Limnerslease
gesso, 1896

CAT 25
Mary Watts reading to G F Watts in the Red Room niche at Limnerslease
Gesso and tempera, c1895
Watts Gallery

CAT 27
MARY SETON WATTS (1849-1938)
George Frederic Watts
Watercolour, dated 'Oct 24th 94'
20.1 x 8.1 cm
Watts Gallery

CAT 28
MARY SETON WATTS (1849-1938)
Entrance Hall Ceiling, Limnerslease
gesso, 1893-98, unf

CAT 29
MARY SETON WATTS (1849-1938)
Tracings from medieval mss for Entrance Hall ceiling, Limnerslease
Pen and ink, 1893
22.6 x 17.5
Watts Gallery

CAT 30
MARY SETON WATTS (1849-1938)
Watts's Studio Fireplace, Limnerslease
terracotta, 1901
100 x 115 cm
Model by Chris Lovell

CAT 31a, b, c
GEORGE FREDERIC WATTS (1817-1904) / SIR EMERY WALKER (1851-1933)
a) *Love and Life*
b) *Love and Death*
c) *Love Triumphant*
Photogravures on Japanese vellum by Sir Emery Walker, 1907, after oil paintings by G F Watts
Watts Gallery

Home Arts and Industries Association, Terra Cotta Home Arts, Guild of Women Binders

Having taught claymodelling to shoeblacks under the Reverend Samuel Barnett's scheme in Whitechapel in 1884-85, Mary met Eglantyne Jebb founder of the handicraft revival movement, the Home Arts and Industries Association. After her marriage Mary was co-opted on to the Home Arts council. She longed to start her own class. When Compton needed a new burial ground, her first thought was to teach villagers to make memorials. The idea of the chapel followed, and Mary founded the Terra Cotta Home Arts at Limnerslease, to train villagers to model its decorative tiles. Like many Arts and Crafts designers, she experimented in a variety of media, sending a design for a bookbinding to be worked by the new Guild of Women-Binders in 1897. Further bookbindings inspired by her designs were exhibited by E Gertrude Farran at Arts and Crafts Exhibition Society exhibitions.

CAT 32
First Exhibition of the Home Arts and Industries Association
photograph, 1885
Lincoln Archives

CAT 33
EGLANTYNE JEBB
Journal
25 June 1886
22.9 x 18.6 cm
Private Collection

CAT 34
The Home Arts and Industries Association leaflet
23.3 x 18.4 cm
Private Collection

CAT 35
Transactions of the National Association for the Advancement of Art and its Application to Industry: Edinburgh Meeting MDCCCLXXXIX
1890
24.5 x 16.5 cm
Watts Gallery
Home Arts aims and developments were aired by leading artists and craftsmen at seminal meetings of the NAAAAI in Edinburgh and Liverpool

CAT 36
MARY SETON WATTS (1849-1938)
An Epsom Beggar
pen and ink, inscribed 'Drawn from Life by the Beggar's Wife, May 30/31, 1895'.
20 x 12 cm
Watts Gallery
Mr and Mrs Watts were spearheading a fundraising campaign for the Home Arts. Here Watts is seen begging for the cause

CAT 37
Home Arts and Industries: Sketches at the Albert Hall
Press cutting from the Watts Collection, 1899
Watts Gallery

CAT 38
MARY SETON WATTS (1849-1938) & THE GUILD OF WOMEN-BINDERS
Bookbinding
leather, 1897
14.3 x 12.1 x 2 cm
Watts Gallery

CAT 39
Exhibition of Book-bindings by the Guild of Women-Binders and the Hampstead Bindery
December 1 1898-30 January 1899
Bernard Middleton

CAT 40
MARY SETON WATTS / E GERTRUDE FARRAN *The Word in the Pattern*
Embossed leather, 1906
EXHIBITED: Grafton Gallery, London, *Arts & Crafts Exhibition Society Exhibition*, 1906, cat 250n
Watts Gallery

CAT 41
The Art Journal 1907 'Gospel at Work' designed by E Gertrude Farran (angels' wings & Cross of hearts inspired by Mary– cf *Thomas à Kempus* 1900 in the National Art Library)

CAT 42
'The Opening Day of the Four Days' Exhibition organised by the Home Arts and Industries Association at the Horticultural Hall'
May 1909
Watts Gallery

Donegal carpet

Commissioned by a fellow Scot, James Morton, Mary designed Liberty's first Celtic-style carpet. *The Pelican* hearth rug was hand-tufted at Killibegs in Donegal for Alexander Morton & Company, Liberty's textile manufacturers. Her design was accompanied by a long letter to be read to the weavers explaining its symbolism. The imagery, characteristic of her Limnerslease and chapel reliefs, included the central 'Heart – symbol of love, the rings at each side the symbol of two strong veins that send a stream of life all over the whole body; the Cross – the four arms made of equal length to show that love must flow all over the earth, from east to west, from north to south. The Dragons – the watchful caretakers of our homes, with wings for quickness. The light and dark chequers – the sign of watchfulness day and night and the sign of life here being between good and evil – joy and sorrow, right and wrong. The T Cross – a key of Eternal Life. The birds at the four corners being the Pelican feeding her birds in distress with her own heart's blood.' Chapel decorations. Mary encouraged Morton to pursue the Celtic style, leading to Liberty's Grafton Gallery exhibition of Irish carpets, 'Founding a National Industry' (1903).

CAT 43
MARY SETON WATTS (1849-1938)
The Pelican
wool, 1899
261.6 x 117 cm
EXHIBITED: 'Founding a National Industry.' Grafton Gallery, London, 1903, cat 17; 'Modern Celtic Art', Grafton Gallery London, 1904
The Wolfsonian, Florida International University

CAT 44
MARY SETON WATTS (1849-1938)
The Pelican
watercolour, stamped 'The Donegal Hand-Made Carpet Patt. & Colour No. A.M. & Co' and inscribed 'Mrs G F Watts Design as shown us by her in Mrs Watts' studio', 1899
56 x 38 cm
Watts Gallery

CAT 45
Letter from Mary Watts to weavers at Alexander Morton & Company's factory at Killibegs, Donegal
20 December 1899
National Archive of Art and Design

CAT 46
Letter from Mary Watts, Limnerslease, to James Morton
15 March 1901
National Archive of Art and Design

The Watts Chapel

A supreme example of the Home Arts ideal, the Watts Chapel was designed by Mary Watts and created by Compton villagers under her guidance. Her model of the chapel was completed in August 1895, classes began in November and the exotic building, covered in terracotta symbolism, carried out in her Celtic / Art Nouveau style, was dedicated on 1 July 1898. So successful was the exterior decorative work that before the interior could be completed, Mary began to transform her terracotta enterprise into a professional business. Watts painted pictures to provide the funding, and a small version of his *All-Pervading* for the altar, but the design and style of the chapel itself was entirely Mary's. However, there are references to Burne-Jones in her spirit figures and medallions in the hands of the cherubim resemble giant Alexander Fisher enamels. In the interior, she was working along similar lines to Phoebe Traquair in Edinburgh, but had not at the time seen Traquair's murals.

CAT 47
MARY SETON WATTS (1849-1938)
Model of Watts Chapel
terracotta, 1895
23 cm high x 20 cm diameter
Watts Gallery

CAT 48
MARY SETON WATTS (1849-1938)
Sketches of details for chapel door in Mrs Watts's journal
pen and ink, 1896
13.3 x 11.2 cm
Watts Gallery

CAT 49
MARY SETON WATTS (1849-1938)
'The Spirit of Hope', The Word in the Pattern
Watts Gallery

CAT 50
GEORGE FREDERIC WATTS (1849-1938)/ SIR EMERY WALKER (1851-1933)
Hope
Photogravure by Emery Walker 1907 after Watts
Watts Gallery

CAT 51
SIR EDWARD COLEY BURNE-JONES (1933-98)
Golden Cup & Golden Greeting
Lithographs from *The Flower Book*, 1904, no 25
16 cm diam
Private Collection

CAT 52
Letter from MSW, Limnerslease
28 January 1920
'Dear Madam, ... You ... will not have failed to see that he was ever decorative!'

CAT 53
The Bishop of Winchester dedicates the Watts Chapel
photograph in Presentation Book, 1 July 1898
43.4 x 28 cm
Watts Gallery

CAT 54
Letter from Mary Watts, Dalcrombie, Stratherrick, to J Gleeson-White
31 July 1898
Watts Gallery

CAT 55
MARY SETON WATTS (1849-1938)
Altar Cross and Candlesticks
brass, inscribed 'WATCHMAN WHAT OF THE NIGHT / THE MORNING COMETH / GIVEN TO THE CHURCH OF ALL SAINTS ENNISMORE GARDENS / IN MEMORY OF / KATHARINE RUSSELL BY HER HUSBAND AND CHILDREN / NOVEMBER 22ND 1905'
110 cm x 30 x 30 cm (cross)
On loan from Holy Trinity Church to the Victoria and Albert Museum

CAT 56
MARY SETON WATTS (1849-1938)
Designs for altar frontal
photograph in pottery manager's album, 1899
Private Collection

CAT 57
MARY SETON WATTS (1849-1938)
The Word in the Pattern
1912
26.3 x 19.7 cm
Watts Gallery

CAT 58
MARY SETON WATTS (1849-1938)
Ideas for symbolism of the interior of the Watts Chapel
pencil, 1898
23.2 x 19.2 cm
Watts Gallery

CAT 59
Mary Watts and Assistants inside the Watts Chapel
photograph, c1904
Watts Gallery

CAT 60
Letter from Phoebe Traquair, 5 Dean Park Crescent, to MSW
1898
Watts Gallery

CAT 61
PHOEBE ANNA TRAQUAIR (1852-1936) / SIR ROBERT LORIMER (1864-1929)
Sanctuary
Silver and enamelled pendant, 1902
Aberdeen Art Gallery and Museum

CAT 62
ALEXANDER FISHER (1864-1936)
The Song of the Storm, Gold and Enamel Morse and *Love Shaking the Rose Tree* in *The Art Journal* 1907

CAT 63
The ashes of G F Watts lying in a casket designed by Mary Watts inside the Watts Chapel,
photograph, July 1904

Silk banners

Earl Grey, Governor-General of Canada, commissioned Mary to design two silk banners for the Canadian people, *Our Lady of the Snows* (1906) was presented by Queen Alexandra to Royal Victoria College, McGill University, and *The Spirit of the Flowers of the Nation* (1907) hung in Government House, Ottawa.

CAT 64
MARY SETON WATTS (1849-1938)
Our Lady of the Snows
mother of pearl, moonstones, rock crystal, garnets, acquamarine, silk and velvet painted, and applied on to satin ground, embroidered with gold and silver thread, 1906
255 x 123 cm
McGill University, Montreal

CAT 65
MARY SETON WATTS (1849-1938)
Banner entry in Journal,
29 July 1906
Watts Gallery

CAT 66
Testament Address to Queen Alexandra for banner 'Our Lady of the Snows'
December, 1903
Watts Gallery

CAT 67 [not exhibited]
MARY SETON WATTS (1849-1938)
The Spirit of the Flowers of the Nation
silk, c1904-6
180 x 70 cm
Presented to Government House, Ottawa, 1907
Victoria & Albert Museum

The Lovat Scouts were founded at Aldourie by Lord Lovat and Mary's brother Ted Fraser Tytler. In 1902, she commissioned Louis Deuchars to design a casket to present to the Lovat Scouts on their return from the Boer War.

CAT 68
MARY SETON WATTS (1849-1938) / LOUIS REID DEUCHARS (1870-1927)
Lovat Scouts Casket
silvered bronze, 1902
inscribed 'FROM THE OFFICERS OF THE FIRST CONTINGENT LOVAT SCOUTS TO CAPTN A.W. McDONALD D.S.O. THE BEST ADJUTANT IN SOUTH AFRICA 1900-1901 LT C STIRLING, L.K.L. McDONALD, COL HONBLE A MURRAY, MAJ. LORD LOVAT D.S.O. CAPT.E.ELLICE LT.I.BRODIE LT.W.T.FRASER-TYTLER CAPT.A.W.McDONALD D.S.O. LT.R.HUNT LT SIR A CAMPBELL-ORDE LT.E.G.FRASER-TYTLER LT.E. GRANT', inscribed on base 'L.R. DEUCHARS DORES 1902' 'FOUNDRY A PARLANTI'
38 x 30 cm
Private Collection

CAT 69
Lovat Scouts Album
Private Collection

The Potters' Arts Guilds at Compton and Aldourie

James Nicol, Mary's first pottery manager, arrived in Compton in January 1901 and remained for 30 years. Apprentice potters were housed in a building designed by Christopher Turnor to double as their hostel and gallery for Watts's paintings. Mary set up a second pottery at Aldourie, which continued until the First World War. Terracotta memorials, garden ornaments and sundials produced to her design were exhibited internationally, won awards, were marketed by Liberty and decorated gardens throughout the country. After Nicol left, George Aubertin managed the Compton pottery until it closed in 1955.

CAT 70
Letter from MSW, Limnerslease, to James Nicol
17 Dec 1900
Private Collection

CAT 71
Laying the Foundation Stone of the Watts Gallery
photograph, 1903
Watts Gallery

CAT 72
CHRISTOPHER TURNOR (1873-1940)
The Hostel and Gallery
Postcard, 1904
Watts Gallery

CAT 73
Mrs Watts's Angels
photograph, 1904
Private Collection

CAT 74
MARY SETON WATTS (1849-1938)
Winged Hours Sundial
terracotta, 1898
92.2 x 32 x 32 cm
EXHIBITED: *Modern Celtic Art*, Grafton Gallery, London, 7-19 March 1903, cat 7
Private Collection

CAT 75
MARY SETON WATTS (1849-1938)
Peacock Sundial
terracotta, 1898
120 x 76 cm
Private Collection

CAT 76
MARY SETON WATTS (1849-1938)
Drawing for 'Utmost' Sundial
1900
23.2 x 17.8 cm
Watts Gallery

CAT 77
George Frederic Watts sitting on 'The Utmost for the Highest' sundial
photograph, c 1901

CAT 78
MARY SETON WATTS (1849-1938)
Martineau Birdbath
terracotta, 1905
91.5 x 50.8 cm
Private Collection

CAT 79
MARY SETON WATTS (1849-1938)
Drawings for Sundials in Mary Watts's Journal
1902
13 x 11 cm
Watts Gallery

CAT 80
MARY SETON WATTS (1849-1938)
Scroll Pot
terracotta, 1898-1902, impressed on body with Compton wheelmark
27.9 x 35.5 cm
Private Collection

CAT 81
MARY SETON WATTS (1849-1938)
Scroll Pot
terracotta, 1898-1902, inscribed on inside 'Cumnock G F SM' impressed with Aldourie wheelmark
27 x 38 cm
Private Collection

CAT 82
Scroll Pot on Celtic stand
terracotta, 1898-1902, stamped 'Compton Pottery'
70.8 x 40 cm
Private Collection

CAT 83
MARY SETON WATTS (1849-1938)
Floreat Pot
terracotta, c1902, inscribed 'T/V', 'ALDOURIE POTTERY DORES'
28 x 32 cm
Inverness Museum & Art Gallery

CAT 84
MARY SETON WATTS (1849-1938)
Eel Pot
terracotta, c1901, impressed with Aldourie mark and inscribed on the inside 'Cumnock G.F.'
49 x 64 cm
Private Collection

CAT 85
MARY SETON WATTS (1849-1938)
Eel Pot
Terracotta prototype, c1898
28.2 x 37 cm
Private Collection

CAT 86
MARY SETON WATTS (1849-1938)
Cobra Pot
terracotta, c1901, inscribed 'IWLD'
27 x 41 cm
Private Collection

CAT 87
MARY SETON WATTS (1849-1938)
Celtic Pot and stand
terracotta, c1899
39.6 x 50 cm
Private Collection

CAT 88
ARCHIBALD KNOX
Brunhild Pot
terracotta, c 1903
stamped 'Designed and Manufactured by Liberty & Co'
24 x 59 x 49 cm
Watts Gallery

CAT 89
ARCHIBALD KNOX / COMPTON POTTERS' ARTS GUILD
Regin Pot on Siegfried pedestal
terracotta, c 1903
stamped 'Designed and Manufactured by Liberty & Co no.15225'
117 x 80 cm
Sweerts de Landas

CAT 90
MARY SETON WATTS
Pedestal Vase
terracotta, c 1901
33.6 x 61.3 cm
Private Collection

CAT 91
Scroll Pots around the fountains in the Central Hall at the Tate Gallery
Illustrated in *The National Gallery of British Art (The Tate Gallery),* Cassell & Co Ltd, London, 1907
Watts Gallery

CAT 92
MARY SETON WATTS (1849-1938)
Bedhead panel
oak, terracotta, tempera, 1901
80 x 30 cm
EXHIBITED: Home Arts and Industries Association, Royal Albert Hall, 1901; *Modern Celtic Art,* Grafton Gallery, London, 7-19 March 1903, cat 26
Watts Gallery

CAT 93
Headstone. illustrated in MRS STEUART ERSKINE Mrs G F Watts' Terra-Cotta Industry
February 1902
Watts Gallery

CAT 94
Country Life
15 March 1902
Private Collection

CAT 95
Book of Garden Ornaments
Liberty & Co, 1904
17 x 12.4 cm
Private Collection

CAT 96
Garden Pottery
Liberty & Co, 1905
14.5 x 22.7 cm
Liberty plc

CAT 97
The Studio Book of Decorative Art
1906-7
29 x 20.2 cm
Private Collection

CAT 98
The Potters' Arts Guild: Mrs G F Watts' Village Industry Compton, Guildford
1 May 1909
18.8 x 12.4 cm
William Morris Gallery

CAT **99**
The Potters' Arts Guild: Mrs G F Watts' Village Industry Compton, Guildford
1 January 1913
18.5 x 12.4 cm
Private Collection

CAT 100
The Potters' Arts Guild
January 1932
20.5 x 15 cm
Watts Gallery

CAT 101a
Royal Horticultural Society Holland House Show medal for Terracotta Garden Ornaments
silver, 1906
3.7 cm diam
Private Collection

CAT 101b
Royal Horticultural Society Holland House Show medal for Terracotta Garden Vases
silver, 1907
5.5 cm diam
Private Collection

CAT 101c
Royal International Horticultural Exhibition London medal
silver, 1912
3.8 cm diam
Private Collection

CAT 101d
Royal Horticultural Society (Chelsea) medal for Terracotta Garden Furniture
silver, 1913
3.7 cm diam
Private Collection

CAT 102
MARY SETON WATTS (1849-1938)
St Louis Pot
Irish clay, 1904
41 x 63.2 cm
Private Collection
In 1902 the Irish Department of Agriculture and Technical Instruction commissioned Mary to make architectural and garden ornaments to show what could be produced from Irish raw materials. This pot was presumably made from Irish clay and among her exhibits in the Irish pavilion at the St Louis World's Fair in 1904

CAT 103
COMPTON POTTERS' ARTS GUILD
Season Pot
Terracotta, c1905
26.8 x 66.5 cm
Private Collection

CAT 104a
ALDOURIE POTTERS' ARTS GUILD
Cherub Box
terracotta, c 1907
18 x 23.5 x 20 cm
Private Collection

CAT 104b
ALDOURIE POTTERS' ARTS GUILD
Cherub Box
terracotta, c 1907
18 x 18 x 36 cm
Private Collection

CAT 105
ALDOURIE POTTERS' ARTS GUILD
Gudrun Pot
terracotta, c 1910, inscribed 'W.D.S.'
18.5 x 30 cm
Private Collection

CAT 106
GERTRUDE JEKYLL (1843-1932) & COMPTON POTTERS' ARTS GUILD
Jekyll Bowl
terracotta, 1908
27.4 x 44.9 cm

CAT 107a & b
COMPTON POTTERS' ARTS GUILD
Pair of Poppy Pots
terracotta, 1908
39.4 x 75 cm, inscribed 'MM'
Private Collection

CAT 108a & b
COMPTON POTTERS' ARTS GUILD
Pair of Duchess Pots & stands
terracotta, c1912
63 x 54 cm
Sweerts de Landas

CAT 109
COMPTON POTTERS' ARTS GUILD
Greek Pot
terracotta, c1912
60 x 44 cm
Private Collection

Cambridge Military Chapel, Aldershot, 1916-21

During the First World War, Mary accepted a commission on behalf of the Guild to decorate the military chapel at Aldershot. Tom Wren modelled the central figure of Christ, but like the other potters was called away for military service. Mary took on the project herself, completing it at the age of 71. Little remains of her Celtic style. The figures are more sculptural than in the Watts Chapel interior, and there is a greater sense of movement in the luscious wings, hands and drapery.

CAT 110
MARY SETON WATTS & TOM WREN
Altarpiece of the Cambridge Military Chapel, Aldershot
gesso, tempera, 1916
86-197.5 cm x 347.5 cm
Watts Gallery

CAT 111
MARY SETON WATTS (1849-1938)
Altar panel from Cambridge Military Chapel, Aldershot
terracotta, painted and overlaid in metal leaf
68 x 49.4 cm
Watts Gallery

CAT 112
COMPTON POTTERS' ARTS GUILD
Miniature pots for Queen Mary's Dolls House
silver, 1923
4 cm high
Private Collection

CAT 113
Letter from Queen Mary's lady-in-waiting regarding pottery fire
silver, 1923
17.7 x 23 cm
Private Collection

CAT 114
Letter from James Nicol to Royle Saywell
Guildford Museum

Compton Potters' Arts Guild Coloured Ware

Decorative household and religious pieces in terracotta, painted in tempera and waxed were impressed with a small circular mark 'P.A.G.' The paper label read 'UNFIRED COLOURS. TO CLEAN OR POLISH USE A HARD BRUSH. DO NOT WASH'. After Mary's death pieces were stamped 'Compton Pottery'

CAT 115
MARY SETON WATTS & TOM WREN
Tending
Terracotta, painted in tempera, 1904
Private Collection

CAT 116
MARY SETON WATTS
St Michael with Archangels
Terracotta plaque, painted in tempera & waxed, c 1904

38.5 x 30.4 x 12 mm
Private Collection

CAT 117
COMPTON POTTERS' ARTS GUILD
Pair of spirits
Terracotta plaques, painted in tempera and waxed, impressed with PAG wheel mark, c 1904
32.2 x 7.6 cm each
Private Collection

CAT 118
COMPTON POTTERS' ARTS GUILD
Sea Nymph
Terracotta bookend, painted in terracotta and waxed, impressed with PAG wheel mark, 1904-10
11 x 7.6 x 11.2 cm
Private Collection

CAT 119
COMPTON POTTERS' ARTS GUILD
St Cecilia
Terracotta figurine, painted in tempera and waxed, 1904-10, impressed with PAG wheel mark
25.6 x 8.8 x 7.5 cm
Private Collection

CAT 120
COMPTON POTTERS' ARTS GUILD
St George
Terracotta plaque, painted in tempera & waxed, c 1904
8.5 x 11 cm wide, impressed with PAG wheel mark
Private Collection

CAT 121
COMPTON POTTERS' ARTS GUILD
St Christopher
Terracotta plaque, painted in tempera & waxed, c 1904
8.5 X 11 cm, impressed with PAG wheelmark
Private Collection

CAT 122
COMPTON POTTERS' ARTS GUILD
St Michael
Terracotta plaque, painted in tempera & waxed, c 1904
19 x 11.5 cm wide, impressed with PAG wheel mark
Private Collection

CAT 123
COMPTON POTTERS' ARTS GUILD
St Michael
Terracotta statuette, painted in tempera, c 1904
Watts Gallery

CAT 124
COMPTON POTTERS' ARTS GUILD
St Francis
Terracotta statuette, painted in green tempera, standing in mahogany box, c 1910
16 x 3.9 x 4.5 cm
Private Collection

CAT 125
COMPTON POTTERS' ARTS GUILD
Iris figurine
one of a series of flower fairies, c 1906
20 cm high
Private Collection

CAT 126
COMPTON POTTERS' ARTS GUILD
St George & the Dragon
Terracotta statuette, painted in tempera, formerly in mahogany box, c 1910, with paper label 'UNFIRED COLOURS: TO CLEAN OR POLISH USE A HARD BRUSH. DO NOT WET.' and impressed with PAG wheel mark
32.5 x 10.3 cm
Private Collection

CAT 127
COMPTON POTTERS' ARTS GUILD
Candlestick lamp
Terracotta, painted in tempera and waxed, c1910
67 x 22 cm
Private Collection

CAT 128
COMPTON POTTERS' ARTS GUILD
Tea Caddy
Beige body, band of relief decoration painted and glazed with vines and 'tea'. Lid with knop of coolie drinking tea, c1910.
13.8 x 8.9 cm
Private Collection

CAT 129
COMPTON POTTERS' ARTS GUILD
Fleur de Lys Vase & lid
Terracotta, painted in tempera and waxed, c1910
47.8 x 18.2 cm
Private Collection

CAT 130
COMPTON POTTERS' ARTS GUILD
Tree of Life Vase & Lid
Terracotta, painted in tempera with sgraffito decoration of Tree of Life, c1910
45.8cm high, 18.8 cm diam
Private Collection

CAT 131
COMPTON POTTERS' ARTS GUILD
Vase & Lid
Terracotta, impressed and painted in tempera with stylized dandelions and sgraffito ribbed decoration to body, c1910
46.8 cm high, 18.8 cm diam
Private Collection

CAT 132
COMPTON POTTERS' ARTS GUILD
Coronation Mug
Terracotta mug, painted in tempera and glazed, celebrating coronation of King George V and Queen Mary, 22 June 1911
12 x 13.5 cm
Private Collection

CAT 133
COMPTON POTTERS' ARTS GUILD
Compton Mug
terracotta, painted in tempera and glazed
11.1 cm high, 9.1 cm diam
Private Collection

CAT 134
COMPTON POTTERS' ARTS GUILD
Pilgrim Bottle
unpainted terracotta, impressed with wheelmark
11 x 10 cm
c 1912
Private Collection

CAT 135
COMPTON POTTERS' ARTS GUILD
Poppy Girl bookend
Terracotta, painted in tempera and waxed
22 x 9.8 cm
Private collection

CAT 136
COMPTON POTTERS' ARTS GUILD
Vine Fruit Platter
Terracotta, painted in tempera & waxed, c1914
32.8 cm diam
Private Collection

CAT 137
COMPTON POTTERS' ARTS GUILD
Hear No Evil, Say No Evil, See No Evil
Terracotta plaque, painted in tempera & waxed, c1920
stamped with PAG wheelmark
15 x 11 cm
Private Collection

CAT 138
COMPTON POTTERS' ARTS GUILD
Elizabeth of Hungary
Terracotta figurine, painted in tempera and waxed, 1920,
28.8 cm x 9.6 cm
Private Collection

CAT 139
COMPTON POTTERS' ARTS GUILD
Miniature Ravenna Casket
terracotta, c1921
9 x 18 cm
Private Collection

CAT 140
COMPTON POTTERS' ARTS GUILD
Miniature garden pots commissioned by Gertrude Jekyll for Queen Mary's Dolls House
terracotta, 1921
Neapolitan clay pot 4.5 x 5.5 cm,
Italian terracotta box 2 x 4 cm
Private Collection

CAT 141
COMPTON POTTERS' ARTS GUILD
Merman candlestick
Terracotta, painted in tempera and waxed
34 x 9.8 cm
Private Collection

CAT 142
COMPTON POTTERS' ARTS GUILD
Sunrise Wave Bookends
Terracotta, painted in tempera and waxed, c1930
17 x 12 cm
Watts Gallery

CAT 143
COMPTON POTTERS' ARTS GUILD
Greek Archer Bookends
Terracotta, painted in tempera and waxed, c1930
18.7 x 17.5 cm
Watts Gallery

CAT 144
COMPTON POTTERS' ARTS GUILD
Lily Pond Platter
Terracotta, painted in tempera & waxed
33 cm diameter
Private Collection

CAT 145
COMPTON POTTERS' ARTS GUILD
Lily Pond Platter
Terracotta, painted in tempera & waxed, 1920s
33 cm diam
Private Collection

CAT 146
COMPTON POTTERS' ARTS GUILD
Butterfly Fruit Bowl
Terracotta, painted in tempera & waxed
10 cm high, 21.5 cm diam
Private Collection

CAT 147
COMPTON POTTERS' ARTS GUILD
Vase
terracotta, painted in green tempera & waxed
28 cm high
Guildford Museum

CAT 148
COMPTON POTTERS' ARTS GUILD
Vase
terracotta, painted in blue tempera and waxed, c1940
stamped 'Compton Pottery Guildford'
19.8 x 18 cm
Watts Gallery

CAT 149
COMPTON POTTERS' ARTS GUILD
Sugar Bowl
terracotta, painted in tempera and waxed
12 cm diam
Watts Gallery

CAT 150
COMPTON POTTERS ARTS GUILD
Vase
Terracotta, painted in green tempera and waxed, c1920
24.5 cm high
Guildford Museum

CAT 151
COMPTON POTTERS' ARTS GUILD
Vase
46.8 cm high, 18.8 cm diam
Private Collection

CAT 153
COMPTON POTTERS' ARTS GUILD
Blue Handled Vase
Terracotta, painted in tempera waxed and stamped with 'Compton Pottery' mark
18.7 high, 16.8 cm high
Private Collection

CAT 152
COMPTON POTTERS' ARTS GUILD
Collection of Pendants, 'Hear No Evil', St Catherine, Cherubs, St Michael on original necklace
Private Collection

CAT 154
COMPTON POTTERS'ARTS GUILD
Potters' Arts Guild
watercolour artwork for advertising
23.4 x 28.2 cm
Private Collection

CAT 155
COMPTON POTTERS' ARTS GUILD
Potters' Arts Guild
Terracotta plaque, painted in tempera and waxed, impressed with PAG wheel mark 1930s 'NOW CLOSED' added later by Wilfrid Blunt, Curator of the Watts Gallery
20 x 25 cm
Watts Gallery

Bibliography

NICOLA GORDON BOWE and ELIZABETH CUMMING, *The Arts and Crafts Movements in Dublin and Edinburgh 1885-1925*, Irish Academic Press, 1998

RONALD CHAPMAN, *The Laurel & the Thorn*, Faber & Faber Ltd, 1945

ELIZABETH CUMMING, *Phoebe Anna Traquair 1852-1936*, Scottish National Portrait Gallery, 1993

CHRISTOPHER FRAYLING, *The Royal College of Art: 150 Years of Art & Design*, Barrie & Jenkins, London, 1987

VERONICA FRANKLIN GOULD, *The Watts Chapel: An Arts & Crafts Memorial*, 1993

ROGER FRY, *Victorian Photographs of Famous Men & Fair Women by Julia Margaret Cameron*, The Hogarth Press, London, 1948

HESTER THACKERAY FULLER, *Tennyson, Watts & Mrs Cameron*, ed Elizabeth Hutchings, Hunnyhill Publications edition, Newport, 1992

GRAFTON GALLERY, LONDON Liberty catalogues 'Founding a National Industry' (1903), 'Modern Celtic Art' (1904)

MALCOLM HASLAM, *Arts & Crafts Carpets,* David Black, London, 1991

JOCELYN MORTON, *Three Generations in a Family Textile Firm*, Routledge & Kegan Paul Ltd, London, 1971

BARBARA MORRIS, *Liberty Design*, Pyramid, Octopus Publishing Group, London, 1989

EDWARD PINNINGTON, *George Paul Chalmers RSA & the Art of His Time* (1838-78), T & R Annan & Sons, Glasgow, 1896

Ed HESTER RITCHIE, *Letters of Anne Thackeeray Ritchie*, 1924

LAURA TROUBRIDGE, *Memories and Reflections*, William Heinemann Ltd, London, 1925

MARY SETON WATTS, *George Frederic Watts: The Annals of an Artist's Life*, Macmillan & Co Ltd, London, 1912, I, 287-88

MARY SETON WATTS, *Journals* (Watts Gallery)

Lenders to the Exhibition

Aberdeen Art Gallery and Museums	cat 61
Guildford Museum	114, 147, 150
Holy Trinity and All Saints Church	55
Inverness Museum and Art Gallery	83
Liberty plc	96
McGill University	64
Bernard Middleton	39
National Archive of Art and Design	46
Sweerts de Landas	89, 108
Trustees of the Victoria and Albert Museum	55
William Morris Gallery	98
The Wolfsonian – Florida International University	
Private Collections	43

Photographic Credits

AIC Studios	page 36c
Graham Bush	17, 57
Roy Fox	2, 21, 24, 25, 38, 60b, 64
Barbara King	53
Liberty	12, 14
Phillips	52
Tate Gallery	46
Peter Turner	29
Trustees of the Victoria & Albert Museum	49, 60
Watts Gallery	22, 31, 32, 41, 44, 58